250+ Essential Phrasal Verbs & Idioms for English Fluency

Follow rapid conversations effortlessly, understand every implied meaning, express yourself naturally, and succeed in any English-speaking situation, personal or professional

Sawsan Charif

Brain Corner Publishing

Copyrights

Contents

Introduction

I magine this: You're sitting in a meeting when the conversation suddenly acceler-ates around you. Your colleague turns and says, "We need to drill down on these numbers, get a ballpark figure, and touch base with the team before we sign off on this project." You smile and nod confidently, but inside, panic rises as you mentally race to translate each phrase. "Drill down", examine in detail? "Ballpark figure", approximate number? "Touch base", communicate briefly? "Sign off", approve? By the time you've decoded the sentence, the conversation has moved on without you.

For non-native English speakers, these moments don't just happen in board-rooms. They happen in team meetings, casual hallway conversations, phone calls, emails, and social gatherings. Each interaction becomes a linguistic obstacle course where idiomatic expressions and phrasal verbs create invisible barriers, not to your intelligence, but to your ability to fully participate, contribute, and connect.

Why Phrasal Verbs and Idioms Are So Difficult

Native English speakers acquire idioms and phrasal verbs gradually over years of immersion, through television, music, family conversations, and school. By the time they enter the workplace, these expressions feel as natural as breathing. For learners of English, however, these same expressions can feel like a secret code that nobody officially teaches you.

The challenge runs deeper than vocabulary. Phrasal verbs and idioms resist literal in-terpretation. "Get the ball rolling" has nothing to do with balls or rolling. "Bite the bullet" involves neither teeth nor ammunition. "Back to the drawing board" doesn't require a pencil. The meaning exists entirely in cultural context, and without that context, even advanced English speakers can find themselves lost.

The four main types of expressions that create communication barriers for English learners are:

• Phrasal Verbs: Verb and particle combinations with non-literal meanings. Examples: "follow up," "sign off," "put together," "call off," "bring up," "take on," "work out"

• Idioms: Fixed expressions with figurative meanings. Examples: "ball is in your court," "back to the drawing board," "hit the ground running," "bite the bullet"

• Cultural References: References tied to sports, history, or American life. Examples: "elevator pitch," "Monday morning quarterback," "hit it out of the park," "full-court press"

• Modern Jargon: Evolving workplace and technology language. Examples: "bandwidth," "circle back," "move the needle," "boil the ocean," "deep dive"

Who This Book Is For

This book is for anyone who uses English in daily life, personally or professionally, and wants to finally feel at home in the language, not just functional in it.

Perhaps you're a skilled professional who understands English grammar perfectly but freezes when native speakers talk quickly and informally. Perhaps you're a student preparing for an English-speaking academic environment. Perhaps you're someone who has lived in an English-speaking country for years but still feels like an outsider in certain conversations. Or perhaps you're a teacher looking for a comprehensive resource to help your students bridge this exact gap.

Whatever your situation, you are not alone. Millions of fluent English speakers around the world share this experience, the frustrating gap between understanding English and truly living inside it.

As a certified ESL teacher and former United Nations conference interpreter with decades of cross-cultural communication experience, I've seen firsthand how mastering these expressions transforms people. Take one of my former students, a brilliant project manager from Brazil, who once confided, "I understand the project perfectly, but I freeze the moment people start throwing idioms around." Her story is not unique. Countless talented, educated, capable individuals find themselves held back not by lack of knowledge, but by a linguistic barrier that nobody warned them about.

That's exactly why I wrote this book.

What This Book Will Do For You

This is not another dry vocabulary list. This is a complete immersion into the living, breathing English that native speakers actually use, with the context, the cultural background, the formality levels, and the practical examples that make the difference between knowing an expression and truly owning it.

By the time you reach the final chapter, you will be able to:

• Follow rapid conversations without losing the thread

• Understand implied meanings, humor, and subtext that go beyond literal words

• Express yourself naturally and confidently using the expressions native speakers reach for instinctively

• Recognize when an expression is formal, informal, or culturally sensitive

• Avoid the common mistakes that signal non-native fluency

• **Adapt your language naturally across different situations, meetings, emails, negotiations, casual conversations, and more**

Before You Begin: Quick Diagnostic

Take two minutes to complete this self-assessment before reading further. For each expression below, rate your confidence level:

1 = I've never heard this expression

2 = I've heard it but I'm not confident using it

3 = I understand it and use it naturally

Rate yourself on each expression:

• "Get the ball rolling" ____

• "Think outside the box" ____

• "Touch base with someone" ____

• "Up to speed" ____

• "The bottom line" ____

• "Call the shots" ____

• "In the loop" ____

• "Take the lead" ____

• "Back to square one" ___

• "Hit the ground running" ___

Your Total Score: ___ / 30

Score Guide:

• **10–16: You're still building your idiom vocabulary, this book will give you a strong, practical foundation.**

• **17–23: You have an intermediate grasp of common expressions, this book will sharpen your confidence and fluency.**

• **24–30: You already have solid idiom knowledge, this book will help you master the subtleties, cultural nuances, and less familiar expressions that will take you to the next level.**

Keep your score in mind as you move through the chapters. You'll return to these same expressions and many more, and by the end, you'll score a confident 30 every time.

How to Use This Book

Each chapter focuses on a specific context, meetings, presentations, networking, written communication, negotiation, leadership, and more. Within each chapter, you'll find:

• Clear explanations of each expression with its meaning and origin

• Multiple examples showing how the expression works across different situations

• Formality indicators so you know when to use an expression and when to avoid it

• Cultural notes that explain the background behind the language

• Interactive exercises to practice and reinforce what you've learned

• Before and After examples showing the difference idioms make in real communication

You don't need to read this book from cover to cover in one sitting. Feel free to jump to the chapters most relevant to your immediate needs. However, if you are building from the ground up, reading sequentially will give you a natural progression from foundational concepts to more advanced application.

A Note on Language and Culture

Language is never neutral. The expressions in this book reflect primarily American English usage, which dominates global business and academic communication. Where British

English equivalents differ significantly, we've noted the distinction. Where expressions carry cultural sensitivity, particularly those rooted in sports, military, or historical references, we've flagged them with context so you can use them with awareness, not just automaticity.

The goal is not for you to sound like someone you're not. The goal is for you to have full access to the language, so that when you choose your words, you're choosing from the complete menu, not just the limited selection available to the uninitiated.

Are you ready? Let's get started.

SPECIAL BONUS!

READY TO MASTER THE TRICKIEST PHRASAL VERBS IN ENGLISH?

Some phrasal verbs have dozens of meanings, and they're often the ones that trip up even advanced learners. As a thank-you for grabbing this book, I'm giving you exclusive access to my Difficult Phrasal Verbs Handbook, your shortcut to finally understanding the phrasal verbs that cause the most confusion.

A preview of what's coming in Volume 2

In this bonus, you'll learn:

- A deep-dive preview on the verb TAKE, one of English's trickiest phrasal verbs
- Real-life example sentences you can use at work, in conversation, and online
- Quick memory tips to help each idiom and phrasal verb stick
- A handy reference you can keep on your phone or print out
- A sneak peek at the business idioms coming in Volume 2

This sneak peek is your exclusive preview of Volume 2. Perfect for ESL learners, business professionals, and anyone who wants to speak English with real confidence.

Click here to download your free guide

Or scan the QR code!

Chapter One

Building a Strong Foundation

You've just started a new job at a multinational company, excited about the opportunities ahead. In your very first meeting, the project lead leans forward and says, "Let's get down to brass tacks, nail this down, and make sure we're not spinning our wheels." You nod along, but inside you're scrambling. "Brass tacks", the essential facts? "Nail this down", finalize it? "Spinning our wheels", wasting time? You understand every individual word, but the sentences feel like a locked room you don't have the key to.

This is the starting point for most English learners in professional environments. Grammar is not the problem, you've studied that. Vocabulary is not the problem, you've built that. The gap is idiomatic fluency: the ability to hear "back to the drawing board" and not picture an architect, or to use "touch base" naturally without feeling like you're performing someone else's language.

This chapter builds the foundation you need, an understanding of what idioms and phrasal verbs actually are, why they work the way they do, and how to begin integrating them into your natural communication.

1.1 The Power of Idioms in Business Communication

Idioms are more than colorful expressions. They are the backbone of nuanced communication, tools that allow speakers to convey complex ideas quickly, warmly, and with precision. When someone says "break the ice," they're not talking about temperature. When they say "get down to brass tacks," no metal is involved. These expressions carry agreed-upon meanings that go beyond the literal words, and they do something plain language often cannot: they create connection.

Consider what happens when a manager says "The ball is in your court" instead of "It's your responsibility now." The idiom does the same informational work, but it also signals a certain cultural ease, a tone of collaboration rather than pressure. It invites rather than instructs. That subtle difference is why native speakers reach for idioms instinctively. They know, without thinking about it, that language is not just about information transfer, it's about relationship.

Key functions of idioms in professional communication:

• Efficiency: Conveys complex meaning in few words. Example: "Let's table this" = postpone discussion until later

• Tone-setting: Signals formality level and relationship. Example: "Shoot me an email" = casual, approachable request

• Inclusion: Creates a shared cultural experience. Example: "We're in the same boat" = we face this together

• Clarity: Cuts through ambiguity in fast discussions. Example: "Bottom line" = the most important point is this

• Cultural signal: Demonstrates fluency and cultural awareness. Example: "Touch base" = shows comfort with informal English

Before idioms: plain language:

"We need to think about this differently and try a new approach because the current plan isn't working."

After idioms: natural fluent English:

"Let's think outside the box here — we need to go back to the drawing board before this gets off the rails."

Both sentences say the same thing. But the second sounds like a native speaker. That's the gap this book closes.

1.2 Understanding Phrasal Verbs: A Business Perspective

If idioms are the paintings of the English language, phrasal verbs are the tools. They are combinations of a verb and one or more particles, prepositions or adverbs, that create a meaning entirely different from the original verb alone. "Turn" is simple. "Turn down" means to reject. "Turn up" means to arrive or increase. "Turn over" means to hand something to someone else. Same verb, three particles, three completely different meanings.

In business communication, phrasal verbs are everywhere. They appear in emails, meetings, presentations, and casual hallway conversations. Understanding them is not optional, it's essential.

The three phrasal verb structures:

Structure 1: Verb + Preposition

Pattern: look + after

Example: "Who's looking after the Henderson account?"

Meaning: To manage or care for

Structure 2: Verb + Adverb

Pattern: scale + back

Example: "We need to scale back the budget by 20%."

Meaning: To reduce in size or scope

Structure 3: Verb + Adverb + Preposition

Pattern: follow + up + on

Example: "Can you follow up on the client proposal?"

Meaning: To check on progress

One critical point: the same verb with different particles produces entirely different meanings. Consider the verb "bring":

• Bring up: Introduce a topic. "I'll bring up the budget issue in the meeting."

• Bring in: Recruit or introduce someone. "We're bringing in a consultant next week."

• Bring forward: Move to an earlier time. "Can we bring the deadline forward by two days?"

• Bring down: Reduce or cause to fall. "We need to bring costs down this quarter."

• Bring on: Cause something to happen. "The new regulations brought on significant changes."

Once you understand the system, you'll start recognizing phrasal verbs not as random expressions to memorize, but as logical combinations to decode.

1.3 Why Context Matters: Using Idioms and Phrasal Verbs Effectively

Knowing an idiom is one thing. Knowing when, where, and with whom to use it is another entirely. Context is the invisible layer that determines whether an idiomatic expression lands perfectly or falls flat, or worse, causes confusion or offense.

Consider "bite the bullet." In an American office, this phrase comfortably signals that someone is accepting an unpleasant situation with resolve. In a more literal-minded cultural context, or with a non-English speaker who has never encountered the expression, the imagery can be genuinely confusing. Same idiom, completely different impact depending on audience.

Four questions to ask before using any idiom or phrasal verb:

1. Is my audience familiar with this expression? If yes: safe to use naturally. If no: explain it or choose a simpler phrase.

2. Is this a formal or informal context? If formal: use formal idioms like "bottom line" or "moving forward." If informal: casual idioms are fine.

3. Does this idiom have cultural references such as sports or military? If yes: add brief context for international audiences. If no: use freely.

4. Am I certain of the meaning in this context? If yes: proceed confidently. If no: paraphrase rather than risk misuse.

Context in action: the same message, two registers:

Email to a senior external client (formal context):

Too casual: "Let's touch base soon and loop you in on our thinking."

Better: "I'd welcome the opportunity to discuss our approach with you at your earliest convenience."

Email to a familiar colleague (informal context):

Too formal: "I would welcome the opportunity to discuss the matter with you."

Natural: "Let's touch base this week — want to loop you in on where we are."

Chapter 1 Practice Exercises

Check your answers in the Answer Key at the back of the book.

Exercise 1: Phrasal Verb Meaning Match

Match each phrasal verb with its correct meaning:

1. Follow up ___

2. Scale back ___

3. Bring forward ___

4. Hand over ___

5. Look into ___

A. Transfer responsibility to someone else

B. Investigate or examine

C. Move a deadline or meeting to an earlier time

D. Reduce the size or scope of something

E. Check on the progress of something

Exercise 2: Formal or Informal?

Decide whether each expression is more appropriate for a formal or informal context. Write F (formal) or I (informal):

1. "Let's circle back on this after the weekend." ___

2. "I would like to revisit this matter at your earliest convenience." ___

3. "I'll shoot you an email with the details." ___

4. "Please find attached the report for your review." ___

5. "We need to get all our ducks in a row before the client call." ___

6. "I would appreciate your feedback on the enclosed proposal." ___

Exercise 3: Real-World Application

Rewrite the following plain-language sentences using an appropriate idiom or phrasal verb:

1. In a team meeting, you want to say the project needs to start over completely.

Your version: ____

2. In an email, you want to say you will check on something and respond later.

Your version: ____

3. In a negotiation, you want to say you are willing to accept less than you originally asked for.

Your version: ____

Chapter Two

Essential Idioms for Meetings

Picture yourself in a boardroom. You've prepared meticulously, slides ready, notes reviewed, talking points memorized. The meeting begins, and the facilitator says: "Let's kick things off by setting the stage for today's discussion. I'd like everyone to feel free to chime in, and once we've broken the ice, we'll open the floor for questions."

Four idioms. One sentence. If you missed even two of them, you've already lost the thread of how this meeting is being framed, before a single agenda item has been discussed.

Meetings are where idiomatic language reaches peak density. Native speakers use these expressions instinctively to open discussions, redirect conversations, manage disagreement, and signal conclusions. This chapter gives you the complete toolkit, with real examples across different meeting types so you can recognize and use these expressions naturally.

2.1 Breaking the Ice: Idioms for Starting Meetings

Opening meeting idioms and their formality levels:

- Kick things off: Begin the meeting or discussion. Formality: Neutral. Best for all meeting types.

- Set the stage: Provide context or background before beginning. Formality: Formal. Best for client meetings and presentations.

• Break the ice: Ease tension and encourage people to open up. Formality: Informal. Best for new teams and first meetings.

• Get the ball rolling: Start the process or discussion moving. Formality: Neutral. Best for brainstorming and project kick-offs.

• Open the floor: Invite others to speak or contribute. Formality: Formal/Neutral. Best for Q&A sessions and team discussions.

• Jump right in: Begin without delay or preamble. Formality: Informal. Best for internal team meetings.

Kick things off: Neutral

Meaning: To begin a meeting or start a discussion

Examples in context:

• Project kickoff: "Let's kick things off by introducing the key stakeholders and outlining our six-month roadmap."

• Weekly standup: "I'll kick things off with the sales numbers before we move to marketing updates."

• Client meeting: "We'd like to kick things off by thanking you for your continued partnership."

Set the stage: Formal / Neutral

Meaning: To provide background context before the main discussion

Examples in context:

• Board meeting: "I'd like to set the stage by sharing the Q3 results that informed today's agenda."

• Training session: "Before we dive in, let me set the stage with some background on why this matters."

• Client presentation: "To set the stage, our company has been working in this space for over fifteen years."

Break the ice: Informal / Neutral

Meaning: To ease tension and create a comfortable atmosphere

Examples in context:

• New team: "To break the ice, let's go around the room and share one thing nobody knows about you."

• First client meeting: "Before we get down to business, perhaps we could break the ice with a quick introduction."

• Virtual meeting: "Since some of us haven't met yet, let's take a moment to break the ice."

Get the ball rolling: Neutral

Meaning: To start something moving: a project, discussion, or process

Examples in context:

• Brainstorming: "To get the ball rolling, I'd like everyone to share one idea — no filtering, just ideas."

• Project launch: "We've done the planning — now it's time to get the ball rolling on execution."

• Negotiation opening: "Let's get the ball rolling. We'd like to propose a three-month pilot program."

2.2 Navigating Discussions: Idioms for Steering Conversations

Even well-planned meetings veer off course. The idioms below are your tools for steering discussions back on track, diplomatically and effectively.

Steering idioms and when to use them:

• Get back on track: Refocus the discussion on the main agenda. Use when conversation drifts to unrelated topics.

• Table the discussion: Postpone a topic to discuss later (US English). Use when a topic needs more time than available.

• Reel it in: Bring a wandering discussion back to the point. Use when debate becomes circular or unfocused.

• Throw it out there: Invite an idea or suggestion into the discussion. Use when encouraging open contribution.

• Chime in: Add to the discussion, contribute a point. Use when inviting quieter members to speak.

• Step up to the plate: Take responsibility or initiative in the meeting. Use when someone needs to lead or decide.

• Take it offline: Continue a detailed discussion outside the meeting. Use when a topic is too complex for current time.

Important cultural note: "Table" means different things:

In American English: "Let's table this" = postpone it, deal with it later.

In British English: "Let's table this" = bring it to the table now, discuss it immediately.

In international meetings, always clarify: "Let's set this aside for now" or "Let's put this on the agenda for next time."

Real meeting dialogue: steering a derailed discussion:

Facilitator: "Before we go further, I want to get us back on track. The budget question is important, but let's take it offline — I'll set up a separate call with the finance team."

Team member: "That works. Can I just throw something out there first? I think there's a faster approach we haven't considered."

Facilitator: "Absolutely — please chime in. And then I'd like Marcus to step up to the plate on the timeline question, since he's been driving that piece."

2.3 Reaching Consensus: Idioms for Agreement and Disagreement

The moment a meeting moves from discussion to decision is where idiomatic language becomes most critical. These expressions help you signal agreement, acknowledge disagreement respectfully, and move toward resolution without damaging relationships.

Agreement and disagreement idioms:

• On the same page: In agreement, sharing the same understanding. Example: "Before we move on, are we all on the same page about the timeline?"

• Seal the deal: Finalize an agreement or decision. Example: "I think we're close — what would it take to seal the deal today?"

• Play devil's advocate: Argue the opposite side to test an idea. Example: "Let me play devil's advocate — what if the timeline is too aggressive?"

• Agree to disagree: Accept that consensus isn't possible, move on respectfully. Example: "We may need to agree to disagree on this one and escalate it."

• Meet halfway: Make mutual concessions to reach compromise. Example: "Can we meet halfway — six weeks instead of four or eight?"

• Find common ground: Identify shared goals or interests between parties. Example: "Let's see if we can find common ground on the core deliverables."

• Move forward: Proceed with a decision, leave the debate behind. Example: "I think we have enough to move forward — let's vote."

Agreement idioms through a full meeting arc:

Opening: "Before we dive in, let's make sure we're all on the same page about today's objective."

Mid-meeting disagreement: "I'll play devil's advocate here — has anyone considered the risk to Q4 revenue?"

Stalled debate: "We may need to agree to disagree on the approach and let the data decide."

Moving toward resolution: "I think we can find common ground if we meet halfway on the budget."

Closing: "Great — I think we're aligned. Let's move forward and I'll send a summary by end of day."

Chapter 2 Practice Exercises

Check your answers in the Answer Key at the back of the book.

Exercise 1: Scenario Matching: Which Idiom Fits Best?

Match each meeting scenario with the most appropriate idiom:

Scenarios:

1. You're opening a meeting with a new client you've never met before. You want to create a relaxed atmosphere. ___

2. The discussion has wandered into a topic that isn't on today's agenda. You need to refocus. ___

3. Two team members have been debating a point for ten minutes with no resolution in sight. ___

4. A negotiation is close to closing. You want to finalize the agreement. ___

5. You want to invite a quiet team member to contribute their perspective. ____

6. A complex issue needs more time than the meeting allows. You want to handle it separately. ____

Idioms:

A. Take it offline

B. Seal the deal

C. Break the ice

D. Agree to disagree

E. Get back on track

F. Chime in

Exercise 2: Fill in the Blank

Complete each sentence with the correct idiom from the box:

Word Box: get the ball rolling / on the same page / play devil's advocate / set the stage / meet halfway / open the floor

1. "Before I _________________, let me _________________ with some background on why we're here today."

2. "Are we all _________________ about the new deadline? I want to make sure there's no confusion."

3. "I'd like to _________________ here — what if the client rejects the proposal entirely?"

4. "We're not going to agree completely, but I think we can _________________ on the budget."

5. "Now I'd like to _________________ for questions — please feel free to ask anything."

Exercise 3: Real-World Role Play

Scenario: You are facilitating a team meeting about a delayed project. Two team members disagree about whose responsibility the delay was. The discussion has gone off topic and time is running short.

Write what you would say in each of the following moments:

1. Bring the conversation back to the agenda. Use: get back on track

Your response:

____

2. Acknowledge both sides without assigning blame. Use: find common ground
Your response:

____

3. Suggest resolving the blame question separately. Use: take it offline
Your response:

____

4. Close the meeting with a clear next step. Use: move forward
Your response:

____

Chapter Three

Idioms for Presentations and Public Speaking

You've prepared for weeks. Your slides are polished, your data is solid, your examples are compelling. You walk to the front of the room, take a breath, and begin. Within thirty seconds, you say something like: "I'd like to paint a picture of where we are today, lay the groundwork for our proposal, and drive the point home by the time we wrap up."

For a native speaker, that sentence flows naturally. For a non-native speaker in the audience, it contains three idioms to decode simultaneously, while also trying to listen to the actual content. And for you as the speaker, using these expressions naturally is the difference between sounding fluent and sounding like you're reading from a script.

This chapter gives you the complete presentation idiom toolkit, from the opening hook to the closing call to action.

3.1 Setting the Stage: Idioms for Opening Presentations

Opening presentation idioms:

- Set the stage: Provide context before the main content. Formality: Formal/Neutral. Best for all presentations.

- Lay the groundwork: Establish the foundation for your argument. Formality: Formal. Best for proposals and reports.

- Hook the audience: Capture attention immediately. Formality: Neutral. Best for any presentation.

- Paint a picture: Create a vivid mental image of the situation. Formality: Neutral. Best for storytelling and strategy.

- Break it down: Explain something complex in simpler terms. Formality: Informal/Neutral. Best for technical presentations.

- Do your homework: Show evidence of thorough preparation. Formality: Neutral. Best for credibility-building.

Set the stage: Formal / Neutral

Meaning: Provide context and framework before the main content

Examples in context:

- Business pitch: "Before I get into the numbers, let me set the stage with a quick overview of the market landscape."

- Training session: "I'd like to set the stage by explaining why this topic matters for everyone in this room."

- Annual report: "To set the stage, our company faced three significant challenges this year — and overcame all three."

Lay the groundwork: Formal

Meaning: Establish the foundation your argument will build on

Examples in context:

- Strategic proposal: "Today I want to lay the groundwork for a three-year digital transformation roadmap."

- Research presentation: "This first section lays the groundwork — without it, the findings won't make full sense."

- Client pitch: "We've spent six months laying the groundwork for this proposal, and today we're ready to share it."

Paint a picture: Neutral

Meaning: Create a vivid, concrete image of a situation or concept

Examples in context:

• Market analysis: "Let me paint a picture of what the market looked like two years ago versus today."

• Problem statement: "To paint a picture — imagine you're a customer trying to navigate our current checkout process."

• Vision statement: "I want to paint a picture of where this company could be in five years if we make these changes."

3.2 Engaging Your Audience: Idioms That Captivate

Engagement idioms and when to use them:

• Keep on the edge of their seats: Maintain suspense and high engagement. Use when building to a key reveal or finding.

• Hit the nail on the head: Make a point with perfect precision. Use when emphasizing the most important insight.

• Connect the dots: Show how separate pieces link together. Use when synthesizing information across sections.

• Spark a dialogue: Invite active discussion and questions. Use when transitioning to Q&A or group discussion.

• Spin a yarn: Tell a compelling story to illustrate a point. Use when introducing a case study or example.

• Bring to life: Make abstract data or concepts feel real and vivid. Use when presenting statistics or complex ideas.

• Unpack: Examine something complex step by step. Use when breaking down a difficult concept.

The storytelling sequence: four idioms in natural flow:

"Let me spin a yarn that brings this data to life. Last year, one of our clients was struggling — and I think their experience really hits the nail on the head when it comes to the problem we're solving. Once I connect the dots between their situation and our solution, I'd love to spark a dialogue about how this might apply to your own context."

Transition idioms: moving between sections smoothly:

• **"Now that we've covered..."**, Use to signal movement to the next section.

• **"Building on that..."**, Use to show how ideas connect.

- **"Let's shift gears"**, Use to move between distinctly different topics.
- **"To connect the dots..."**, Use to synthesize ideas before moving on.
- **"The bottom line is..."**, Use to state the key takeaway before transitioning.
- **"Let's zoom out / zoom in"**, Use to move between big picture and detail.

3.3 Leaving a Lasting Impression: Closing with Impact

Drive the point home: Neutral

Meaning: Reinforce the core message so it sticks

Examples in context:

- Sales pitch close: "Let me drive the point home — every week we delay costs us approximately $40,000 in lost revenue."
- Training conclusion: "I want to drive this point home before we finish: consistency matters more than intensity."
- Executive summary: "To drive the point home — these three changes alone would transform our customer retention rate."

Bring it full circle: Neutral / Formal

Meaning: Return to the opening to create a cohesive narrative

Examples in context:

- Story-based presentation: "Let me bring this full circle — remember the client story I opened with? Here's where they are today."
- Problem-solution structure: "To bring it full circle: we started with a problem, and we're ending with a proven solution."
- Annual review: "I'd like to bring us full circle to the three goals we set at the start of the year."

Plant a seed: Neutral

Meaning: Leave the audience with an idea that will grow over time

Examples in context:

• Innovation talk: "I'm not here to give you all the answers today. I'm here to plant a seed — one that I hope will grow into action."

• Leadership presentation: "What I hope to plant a seed of today is the idea that small habits drive extraordinary outcomes."

• Conference keynote: "If I've planted even one seed today — one question you'll keep thinking about — this talk has done its job."

Complete presentation arc: idioms from open to close:

• **Opening:** "I want to open with a question that might surprise you.", Hook the audience

• **Context:** "To set the stage — eighteen months ago, this company was losing market share.", Set the stage

• **Foundation:** "First, let me lay the groundwork by defining what we mean by grow th.", Lay the groundwork

• **Illustration:** "Let me paint a picture of what success looks like at the eighteen-month mark.", Paint a picture

• **Key insight:** "This chart hits the nail on the head — cost is not the issue. Speed is.", Hit the nail on the head

• **Synthesis:** "Now let me connect the dots between everything we've covered.", Connect the dots

• **Closing:** "To drive the point home — one decision today changes everything.", Drive the point home

• **Call to action:** "I'll leave you with this thought — a seed I hope you'll carry forward.", Plant a seed

Chapter 3 Practice Exercises

Check your answers in the Answer Key at the back of the book.

Exercise 1: Match the Presentation Stage

Match each idiom to the stage of a presentation where it fits best:

1. "Let me paint a picture of the challenge we're facing." ___

2. "To bring it full circle — remember the story I opened with?" ___

3. "Let's shift gears and move into the financials." ___

4. "I want to drive this point home before we close." ___

5. "Let me lay the groundwork before we dive into solutions." ___

Stages:

A. Conclusion / Reinforcement

B. Transition between sections

C. Opening context / Problem framing

D. Foundation building

E. Final closing

Exercise 2: Complete the Presentation Script

Fill in the blanks using the idioms in the box:

Word Box: paint a picture / connect the dots / hit the nail on the head / plant a seed / set the stage

"Good morning everyone. I'd like to _________________ for today's discussion by sharing three trends that are reshaping our industry. Let me _________________ of where the market stood just two years ago versus today. As we go through each section, we'll _________________ between past, present, and future. I think our research _________________ when it shows that customer expectations have shifted permanently — not temporarily. And if nothing else, I hope today's session _________________ — an idea you'll keep thinking about long after you leave this room."

Exercise 3: Write Your Own Opening

You are presenting a proposal to introduce a new employee wellness program at your company. Write a 4–6 sentence opening using at least three idioms from this chapter. Your opening should hook the audience, set the stage for what the presentation will cover, and establish your credibility or the groundwork for your proposal.

Your opening:

____

____

____

Exercise 4: Cultural Sensitivity Check

Some presentation idioms work well with all audiences. Others require cultural context. For each idiom below, decide: Safe for international audiences (S) or Needs context / explanation (N):

1. "This is a real home run for our team." ____
2. "Let's connect the dots." ____
3. "We knocked it out of the park." ____
4. "Let me paint a picture." ____
5. "We need to move the goalposts." ____
6. "To drive the point home..." ___

Phrasal Verbs for Professional Networking

You're at an industry conference. The room is buzzing. Someone you've been wanting to meet walks over and introduces themselves. The conversation starts well, until they say: "I've been trying to break into your sector for a while. Would love to pick your brain sometime. Maybe we can get together and I'll loop in my colleague who's also looking to reach out to companies like yours."

Four phrasal verbs in two sentences. If any of them missed you, the conversation's subtext has already slipped past: they want to enter your industry, get your informal advice, meet up, and include a colleague. That's a lot of information, and a lot of relationship-building, carried entirely by phrasal verbs.

Networking is where phrasal verbs carry the heaviest load. This chapter gives you the complete phrasal verb toolkit for every stage of the networking relationship: initiating, maintaining, and following up.

4.1 Making Connections: Phrasal Verbs for Initiating Relationships

Networking initiation phrasal verbs:

- Reach out to: Contact someone to initiate a connection. Formality: Neutral. Context: Email, LinkedIn, calls.
- Break into: Enter a new industry or field. Formality: Neutral. Context: Career conversations.
- **Hit it off:** Connect instantly and naturally with someone. Formality: Informal. Context: Networking events.
- **Get together:** Meet up, arrange a meeting or coffee. Formality: Informal. Context: Follow-up invitations.
- **Pick someone's brain:** Ask for informal advice or insights. Formality: Informal. Context: Mentorship, information gathering.
- **Get in touch:** Make contact: neutral and widely understood. Formality: Neutral. Context: All contexts, all cultures.
- **Link up with:** Connect professionally, often digitally. Formality: Neutral. Context: LinkedIn, introductions.
- Come across: Encounter or discover someone unexpectedly. Formality: Neutral. Context: Casual encounters, online.

Reach out to: Neutral

Meaning: To contact someone with the intent to connect or start a conversation

Examples in context:

- LinkedIn message: "I wanted to reach out after seeing your talk at the summit last week — your insights on market entry really resonated."
- Email introduction: "I'm reaching out because a mutual colleague, Priya Sharma, suggested we might have a lot to discuss."
- Conference follow-up: "It was great meeting you yesterday — I'm reaching out to see if you'd be open to a follow-up conversation."

Pick someone's brain: Informal

Meaning: To ask someone for their informal expertise, advice, or perspective

Examples in context:

- Mentorship request: "I'd love to pick your brain about how you transitioned from consulting into product management."

- Industry insight: "Would you have twenty minutes for a quick call? I'd love to pick your brain about the regulatory landscape."
- Career advice: "I'm at a crossroads and would really value the chance to pick your brain — you've navigated this exact situation before."

Break into: Neutral

Meaning: To successfully enter a new industry, field, or professional circle
  Examples in context:
- Career pivot: "I've been working in finance for eight years and I'm looking to break into the sustainability sector."
- New market: "We're trying to break into the Southeast Asian market and looking for local partners."
- Industry networking: "It took me two years to really break into the tech startup ecosystem, but this conference helped enormously."

4.2 Maintaining Rapport: Phrasal Verbs for Sustaining Connections

Making a connection is the easy part. Keeping it alive over weeks, months, and years is where most networking falls apart. The phrasal verbs below are your tools for staying present, relevant, and genuinely connected.

  Rapport maintenance phrasal verbs:
- **Keep in touch:** Maintain regular contact over time. Use when parting, signals ongoing commitment.
- **Catch up with:** Reconnect after a period without contact. Use after a gap of weeks or months.
- **Check in on:** Show interest in someone's progress or wellbeing. Use periodically, shows genuine investment.
- **Follow through on:** Deliver on a promise or commitment made earlier. Use always, reliability defines professional reputation.
- **Loop in:** Include someone in a conversation or project. Use when expanding a discussion or collaboration.

• **Stay connected:** Maintain the relationship actively. Use when closing any meeting or networking interaction.

• **Build on:** Develop a relationship or conversation further. Use after a strong initial interaction.

The relationship maintenance sequence:

When you meet someone: "It was wonderful meeting you — let's keep in touch."

One week later: "Just wanted to follow through on our conversation and send over that article I mentioned."

One month later: "Checking in — how did the product launch go?"

Three months later: "Would love to catch up — a lot has happened since we last spoke."

When relevant: "I'm looping you in on a project that I think aligns perfectly with what you described."

4.3 Following Up: Keeping the Momentum Going

A warm lead that isn't followed up becomes a cold contact within two weeks. The follow-up is where most networking investment is lost, not because people don't intend to follow up, but because they don't know how to do it without sounding pushy, awkward, or formulaic.

Follow-up phrasal verbs:

• Follow up on: Check on or continue a previous discussion. Example: "I wanted to follow up on our conversation from Tuesday."

• Touch base: Make brief contact to stay connected or update. Example: "Just touching base to see if you had a chance to review the proposal."

• Circle back: Return to a topic or person after a pause. Example: "Let me circle back to you once I've spoken with the team."

• Get back to: Respond to someone after gathering information. Example: "I'll get back to you by end of week with a decision."

• Reach back out: Re-initiate contact after a period of silence. Example: "I'm reaching back out — I know it's been a while since we connected."

• Move forward: Take the next step in a relationship or project. Example: "I'd love to move forward — what does your calendar look like next week?"

Email templates: follow-up phrasal verbs in action:

Template 1: After a networking event:

Subject: Great meeting you at [Event Name]

Hi [Name],

It was wonderful connecting with you yesterday. I wanted to reach out while the conversation was still fresh. The work you described on supply chain resilience really resonated with some challenges we're navigating.

I'd love to get together for a coffee or a short call when your schedule allows, I'd genuinely enjoy the chance to pick your brain further, and I think there could be some interesting overlap in what we're each working on.

Looking forward to staying connected.

[Your Name]

Template 2: Reconnecting after a long gap:

Subject: Reaching back out: long overdue!

Hi [Name],

I'm reaching back out after way too long: I hope the past few months have been good to you. I've been following your company's expansion into the European market and wanted to check in and congratulate you.

I'd love to catch up properly. A lot has changed on my end too, and I think we'd have a great conversation. Would you be open to a quick call sometime in the next few weeks?

Hope to hear from you soon.

[Your Name]

Template 3: Following up after sharing a resource:

Subject: Following up: the report I mentioned

Hi [Name],

Just following up on our conversation from last week, I wanted to make sure I followed through on sending you that industry report I mentioned. I've attached it here.

Let me know what you think when you get a chance to look through it. I'd be happy to circle back after you've had time to review and talk through the implications for your market.

Hope it's useful.

[Your Name]

Chapter 4 Practice Exercises

Check your answers in the Answer Key at the back of the book.

Exercise 1: Phrasal Verb in Context

Choose the most appropriate phrasal verb to complete each networking sentence:

1. "I'd love to _____________________ your brain about how you made the transition to consulting." (pick / reach / loop)

2. "I'm _____________________ to introduce myself after seeing your article in Harvard Business Review." (reaching out / breaking into / hitting off)

3. "Let's _____________________ next month — I'd love to hear how the new role is going." (catch up / follow through / come across)

4. "I wanted to _____________________ on our conversation and send over the contact I promised." (follow up / touch base / circle back)

5. "Could you _____________________ Maria on this email thread? She's been working on a similar project." (loop in / break into / get together)

Exercise 2: Write Your Elevator Pitch

Draft a 4–6 sentence elevator pitch using at least three phrasal verbs from this chapter. Your pitch should introduce who you are and what you do, express what you're looking to achieve or explore, and invite a connection or next step.

Your pitch:

____

____

____

Exercise 3: Write a Follow-Up Email

You met a potential mentor at a conference last week. They work in your target industry and suggested you reach out. Write a short follow-up email using at least four phrasal verbs from this chapter. Include a reference to where you met, a specific reason for reaching out, and a clear low-pressure invitation to connect further.

Your email:

____

____

____

Exercise 4: Cultural Nuance Check

For each expression below, identify whether it is Safe for all international contexts (S) or May need adaptation (A):

1. "Can I pick your brain for a few minutes?" ___

2. "I'd like to get in touch about a potential opportunity." ___

3. "Let's touch base next week." ___

4. "I'm reaching out to follow up on our meeting." ___

5. "I was hoping to pick up where we left off." ___

Chapter Five

Cultural Insights and Origins

Imagine stepping into a meeting where someone advises, "Let's not jump the gun." You nod, but inside you're dissecting the phrase, wondering about its origins and what it truly means in this context. Language, especially in professional environments, is peppered with idioms that hold more than their surface meaning. They are echoes of history, reflections of culture, and often, they encapsulate entire narratives within a few words.

Understanding these idioms is not just about language proficiency. It's about grasping the cultural stories they tell, stories that help you navigate professional environments with greater ease, confidence, and genuine fluency.

5.1 The Cultural Roots of Business Idioms

Many idioms have their roots in historical events, industries, or cultural practices that have long since faded. Yet the expressions live on, carrying their original weight into modern conversations. Knowing where an idiom comes from doesn't just satisfy curiosity, it helps you remember it, use it correctly, and recognize when it might not land with certain audiences.

Common business idioms and their surprising origins:

- **Bite the bullet:**

Origin: military.

Before anesthesia, soldiers were given bullets to bite during painful procedures. Meaning today: accept something unpleasant and get through it without complaint. Example: "We're going to have to bite the bullet and cut the budget by fifteen percent."

- **Burn the midnight oil:**

Origin: pre-electricity era.

Oil lamps were used for late-night work sessions. Meaning today: work late into the night, especially on something important. Example: "The team burned the midnight oil to finish the proposal before the deadline."

- **All hands on deck:**

Origin: nautical.

Every sailor was required on deck during a crisis at sea. Meaning today: everyone is needed, all resources must be deployed immediately. Example: "With the product launch tomorrow, it's all hands on deck."

- **Reap what you sow:**

Origin: agriculture.

A direct reference to farming, you harvest what you plant. Meaning today: the results you get reflect the effort and choices you put in. Example: "We invested heavily in customer service and our retention numbers show it — you reap what you sow."

- **Pull yourself up by your bootstraps:**

Origin, American frontier culture.

Originally used ironically to describe an impossible task, it evolved to represent self-reliance. Meaning today: achieve success through your own effort without outside help. Example: "He came to this country with nothing and built a company from scratch — a true example of pulling yourself up by your bootstraps."

- **Hit the ground running:**

Origin: military and parachuting.

Soldiers landing in enemy territory needed to start moving immediately. Meaning today: begin something with energy and momentum, without needing time to warm up. Example: "We need someone who can hit the ground running — no time for a long onboarding."

- **On the same wavelength:**

Origin: radio technology.

Two radios tuned to the same frequency could communicate. Meaning today: two people who think alike, understand each other intuitively. Example: "We've been working together so long we're on the same wavelength — barely need to explain things."

Why origins matter for language learners:

When you understand where an idiom comes from, three things happen. First, the meaning becomes logical rather than arbitrary, "all hands on deck" makes perfect sense once you picture a ship in a storm. Second, the imagery helps you remember it, you'll never confuse "bite the bullet" with another expression. Third, you understand the emotional weight, these aren't neutral phrases. They carry connotations of bravery, hard work, urgency, or self-reliance that the literal words don't capture.

5.2 Understanding Regional Variations in Idiomatic Expressions

Imagine you're at an international business conference. You're deep in conversation with a colleague from the UK when they casually say, "Well, Bob's your uncle." You pause. In British English, this means "and there you have it", a simple completion of a task. To an American English speaker, it sounds completely foreign. This is the challenge of regional idioms in global professional settings.

The same English language produces entirely different idiomatic vocabularies depending on the country. What feels natural and obvious to a British speaker can baffle an American, Australian, or Singaporean colleague, and vice versa.

American vs. British idioms: side by side:

• **"Touch base" (American) vs. "Have a word" (British)**: Both mean to make brief contact, but the American version is used more casually. An American manager saying "let's touch base" may surprise a British colleague who expects only a very brief check-in rather than a full update meeting.

• **"Ballpark figure" (American) vs. "Rough estimate" (British):**
The American version draws on baseball, the approximate size of a ballpark. British colleagues may understand it but would not use it naturally.

• **"Monday morning quarterback" (American) vs. "Armchair critic" (British):**
Both describe someone who criticizes decisions after the fact. The American version requires knowledge of American football, in international meetings, it often falls flat or causes confusion.

• **"Take a rain check" (American) vs. "Take a pass for now" (British):**

The American version means politely declining but leaving the door open for later. British colleagues may not use this expression naturally.

• **"Bob's your uncle" (British) vs. No direct American equivalent:**

This British expression meaning "and it's done" or "simple as that" has no natural American counterpart, and will puzzle most American professionals.

• **"Flat out like a lizard drinking" (Australian) vs. "Slammed" or "Swamped" (American/British):**

The Australian expression vividly describes being extremely busy. It is charming and vivid, and completely opaque to anyone outside Australia.

Key principle for international professionals:

When you're speaking with someone whose regional English background you don't know, default to the most universally understood expression. "Get in touch" is safer than "touch base." "Rough estimate" is safer than "ballpark figure." "Working hard" is safer than "flat out like a lizard drinking." Reserve the more culturally specific expressions for audiences you know well.

5.3 American Business Culture: Idioms You Need to Know

American business culture is characterized by directness, a bias toward action, a celebration of innovation, and a strong emphasis on results. The idioms that dominate American workplaces reflect all of these values. Understanding them is not just linguistic, it's cultural.

Core American business idioms and the values they reflect:

• **Think outside the box:**

Value: innovation and creativity. Invites unconventional thinking, challenging the status quo.

Example: "We've tried the standard approach. Let's think outside the box — what would we do if there were no constraints?"

• **Raise the bar:**

Value: ambition and excellence. Setting higher standards, pushing beyond what was previously considered sufficient. Example: "Last year's results were strong, but this year we want to raise the bar even further."

• **Win-win situation:**

Value: collaboration and mutual benefit.

Reflects a preference for outcomes where all parties gain.

Example: "I think this partnership is a genuine win-win — our distribution network and their technology fill each other's gaps perfectly."

- **Game changer:**

Value: transformation and impact.

Describes something that fundamentally alters the landscape. Example: "This technology isn't just an improvement — it's a game changer for the entire logistics sector."

- **Move the needle:**

Value: measurable results and accountability.

Means to make a noticeable difference, to shift outcomes in a meaningful way.

Example: "We've run three campaigns this quarter, but none of them have really moved the needle on brand awareness."

- **Show me the money:**

Value: results and tangible outcomes. Demands proof of financial or practical results.

Example: "The concept sounds great, but our investors are saying show me the money — they want revenue projections."

- **Bang for your buck:**

Value: efficiency and return on investment. Getting maximum value from an expenditure.

Example: "In terms of bang for your buck, email marketing still outperforms almost every other channel."

- **The bottom line:**

Value: financial focus and directness. The most important point, especially financial.

Example: "The bottom line is that we cannot sustain these losses beyond Q3."

How American media spreads these idioms globally:

American films, television series, business podcasts, and social media have exported American idioms to every English-speaking and English-learning community in the world. Expressions like "game changer," "think outside the box," and "the bottom line" now appear regularly in business conversations in Germany, Brazil, Japan, and beyond, often used by non-native speakers who absorbed them from American content. This global spread means these American idioms are increasingly understood worldwide, making them safer to use in international settings than more regionally specific expressions.

Chapter 5 Practice Exercises

Check your answers in the Answer Key at the back of the book.

Exercise 1: Match the Origin

Match each idiom to its historical or cultural origin:

1. "All hands on deck" ___

2. "Burn the midnight oil" ___

3. "Bite the bullet" ___

4. "Reap what you sow" ___

5. "Hit the ground running" ___

Origins:

A. Agriculture and farming

B. Military combat before modern medicine

C. Naval seafaring

D. Pre-electricity lamp-lit work sessions

E. Military parachute operations

Exercise 2: American or British?

Identify whether each expression is primarily American English (A), British English (B), or used in both (Both):

1. "Touch base" ___

2. "Bob's your uncle" ___

3. "The bottom line" ___

4. "Take a rain check" ___

5. "Move the needle" ___

6. "Ballpark figure" ___

7. "Think outside the box" ___

Exercise 3: Safe for International Use?

You are presenting to a mixed international audience. Decide whether each expression is Safe (S) to use without explanation, or Needs context (N):

1. "We need to raise the bar this quarter." ____
2. "This is a real Monday morning quarterback situation." ____
3. "The bottom line is we need a decision today." ____
4. "Let's not jump the gun." ____
5. "It's all hands on deck until the launch." ____
6. "We knocked it out of the park." ____

Exercise 4: Origins Research Exercise

Choose one idiom from the list below that you find most interesting. Research its historical roots using an online etymology dictionary such as etymonline.com. Write a short paragraph of 4–6 sentences explaining where the idiom comes from and how that origin connects to its modern business meaning.

Idioms to choose from:
- "Spill the beans"
- "No room to swing a cat"
- "Barking up the wrong tree"
- "Costs an arm and a leg"
- "Bite off more than you can chew"

Your research paragraph:

____

____

____

Exercise 5: Rewrite for International Audiences

Rewrite each sentence by replacing the culturally specific idiom with a more universally understood expression:

1. "This new strategy is a real game changer — we knocked it out of the park."
Your version:

____

2. "Let's touch base after the weekend and make sure we're all on the same page."

Your version:

____

3. "Bob's your uncle — just submit the form online and you'll have access within minutes."

Your version:

____

Loving the Book So Far?

If the first few chapters have already given you an "aha!" moment, helped a tricky phrasal verb finally click, or shown you the cultural story behind an expression you've heard for years, I have a small favor to ask.

Honest reviews from readers like you are the single most important way new readers discover this book. Even a quick sentence or two helps another English learner decide that this might be the book that finally bridges the gap between understanding English and truly living inside it.

Your review doesn't need to wait until you've finished. If you're finding value already, share what's working for you so far. It would mean the world to me, and honestly, it's the most powerful way to help other readers find this book.

Take a quick moment here:

sawsancharif.com/review

Scan to Review

Chapter Six

Overcoming Common Challenges

You find yourself in a conference room when someone says, "Let's not bark up the wrong tree on this one." You pause. Is that a criticism of the current approach? A warning? A suggestion? You nod cautiously, but inside you've already lost the thread.

This is one of the most frustrating experiences for non-native English speakers, not the big vocabulary words, not the grammar, but the idioms that fly past before you've had a chance to decode them. And the frustration compounds: you don't want to stop the meeting to ask, so you stay silent, and the moment passes.

This chapter is dedicated to the practical challenges of learning and using idioms, building confidence, avoiding misinterpretation, and creating a learning practice that actually sticks.

6.1 Boosting Confidence: Using Idioms Without Fear

The single biggest barrier most non-native speakers face isn't knowledge, it's confidence. You may know an idiom perfectly. You may have studied it, written it down, seen it used in context. And then the moment arrives to use it in a real conversation, and something holds you back.

This hesitation is completely normal. Here's what's actually happening:

• You're worried the idiom will sound forced or unnatural coming from you

- You're not one hundred percent certain you're using it in exactly the right context
- You're afraid of the reaction if you get it slightly wrong
- You're performing in a second language in a high-stakes environment

All of these concerns are valid. And all of them dissolve with one thing: deliberate, low-stakes practice before the high-stakes moment arrives.

The One Idiom Per Week Method

The most effective approach for building idiomatic confidence is not to study fifty expressions at once. It's to choose one idiom per week and use it deliberately until it feels owned rather than borrowed.

Here's how it works:

Step 1: Choose one idiom from this book that fits your current work context. Don't choose randomly. Choose one you'll actually have an opportunity to use this week.

Step 2: Write it down with its meaning, its formality level, and two or three example sentences that fit your specific work situation.

Step 3: Use it at least three times this week. Once in writing, an email or message. Once in a meeting or conversation. Once when explaining something to a colleague informally.

Step 4: Notice the reaction. Did anyone respond to it? Did it land naturally? Did you feel it fit?

Step 5: At the end of the week, decide: is this expression now part of your natural toolkit? Or does it need more practice?

After twelve weeks using this method, you'll have twelve expressions that genuinely feel like yours. That's more progress than memorizing two hundred expressions you never use.

Success Looks Like This

A project manager from Mexico once confided that she avoided all idioms in meetings because she was afraid of using them incorrectly. She started with just one: "Let's take this offline." She used it in a meeting when a discussion started to derail. Her colleagues responded naturally, the meeting moved on, and she felt, for the first time, that her English was something she was doing rather than something being done to her.

That shift: from passive understanding to active ownership, is what deliberate practice creates.

Practical Confidence Strategies

• Start with high-frequency, low-risk expressions: "touch base," "follow up," "circle back," "take it offline", these are used constantly and carry almost no risk of misinterpretation

• Pair a new idiom with something you already say confidently, so the familiar language carries the unfamiliar

• Prepare two or three idioms before any important meeting so they're ready to use naturally rather than searched for in the moment

• When an idiom doesn't land perfectly, don't freeze, simply continue speaking. Native speakers mishear and misuse expressions too. The conversation moves on.

6.2 Avoiding Misinterpretations: Navigating Tricky Idioms

Some idioms are so vivid that non-native speakers visualize them literally, and the image makes no sense. "Barking up the wrong tree" conjures a dog at a tree. "Cut to the chase" suggests a physical pursuit. "Bite the bullet" is genuinely alarming if you don't know the military origin.

Misinterpretation happens in two directions: you misunderstand an idiom someone uses, or you use an idiom whose meaning others misread. Both are solvable with the right strategies.

The Most Commonly Misunderstood Business Idioms

• "Bark up the wrong tree": Does NOT mean to make noise or cause trouble. Means: to pursue a mistaken or misguided course of action, to look for something in the wrong place. Example: "We've been trying to fix the interface, but I think we're barking up the wrong tree — the problem is in the backend code."

• "Cut to the chase": Does NOT mean to move quickly or make a hasty decision. Means: to get to the main point without unnecessary preamble. Origin: early film editing, cutting to the exciting chase scene. Example: "I'll cut to the chase — we're over budget and we need to decide today."

- "Hit the wall": Does NOT always mean to stop completely. Often means: to reach a point of exhaustion or difficulty where progress feels impossible. Example: "The team has hit the wall on this project — we need a fresh perspective."

- "Spill the beans": Does NOT mean to make a mess. Means: to reveal a secret, often accidentally. Example: "Don't spill the beans about the merger before the official announcement."

- "Sit on the fence": Does NOT mean to be comfortable or neutral. Means: to avoid committing to a position, often when a decision is needed. Example: "We can't sit on the fence any longer — a decision needs to be made by Friday."

- "Under the weather": Does NOT mean outdoors or exposed to elements. Means: feeling unwell, not at full strength. Example: "I'm a bit under the weather today — I may need to keep the meeting short."

- "In hot water": Does NOT mean literally warm. Means: in trouble, facing serious consequences. Example: "The company is in hot water with regulators after last quarter's report."

- "Go back to the drawing board": Does NOT mean to draw or sketch. Means: to start over completely because the current approach has failed. Example: "The prototype failed every test — we need to go back to the drawing board."

When You Don't Understand an Idiom: What to Do

The most professional response to not understanding an idiom is not to pretend, it's to ask naturally. Here are three ways to do it without breaking the flow of conversation:

- **"Just to make sure I'm following:** when you say [idiom], you mean [your interpretation]?",

This signals you're engaged and checking your understanding, not confused.

- **"Could you say more about what you mean by that?",**

Open-ended, keeps the conversation moving, works in any professional context.

- **After the meeting:**

"Quick question - when [name] said [idiom] earlier, I want to make sure I understood correctly. Did they mean...?",

Low-stakes clarification that shows diligence.

What not to do: sit through an entire meeting having missed a key phrase, make decisions based on a misunderstood idiom, or feel embarrassed about asking. Every professional, in every language, asks clarifying questions.

6.3 Overcoming the Fear of Mistakes: Practicing Idioms Safely

Mistakes are not the problem. Avoiding practice because of fear of mistakes, that's the problem. Every fluent English speaker has used an idiom slightly incorrectly, in the wrong context, or with the wrong audience. The language absorbs it. The conversation continues.

What separates confident idiomatic speakers from hesitant ones is not perfection, it's volume of practice. The more often you use expressions in low-stakes settings, the more naturally they emerge in high-stakes ones.

Three Safe Practice Environments

Environment 1: Your own writing:

Email is your safest practice ground. Before sending any professional email, challenge yourself to include one idiom from the chapter you've most recently studied. Writing gives you time to think, check, and revise. Over time, the expressions that start in your written language migrate naturally into your spoken language.

Environment 2: One-on-one conversations:

A one-on-one meeting with a trusted colleague is far less intimidating than a group meeting. This is where to try out a new idiom for the first time. If it doesn't land perfectly, the feedback is immediate and private.

Environment 3: Your own language journal:

Keep a small notebook or digital document where you record idioms you've encountered, used, or want to use. After each week, review what you tried. Did it work? Did anyone react to it? What would you do differently? This reflection accelerates learning significantly.

Your Idiom Integration Checklist

Use this checklist each week to build your practice habit:

1. Choose one idiom to focus on this week. Write it down with its meaning and two example sentences from your own work context.

2. Use it in writing: an email, a message, a document, at least once.

3. Use it in a spoken conversation: a meeting, a call, a casual exchange, at least once.

4. Note the reaction. Did it fit naturally? Did anyone respond to it?

5. Ask for feedback from a trusted colleague or language partner if possible.

6. At week's end, reflect: is this expression now yours? Or does it need another week?

The Growth Mindset for Language Learners

Every expert in any language: including their native one, makes mistakes with idioms. Expressions get mixed up: "I'll burn that bridge when I come to it" instead of "cross that bridge." "We're skating on thin water" instead of "thin ice." Native speakers do this constantly. It's called a malapropism, and it happens to everyone.

When you make a mistake with an idiom:

• Don't stop speaking. Continue the sentence as if you meant it.

• If someone looks confused, paraphrase quickly: "What I mean is..."

• Note what happened afterward and adjust for next time.

• Keep going. The only real mistake is stopping practice because of the fear of mistakes.

Chapter 6 Practice Exercises

Check your answers in the Answer Key at the back of the book.

Exercise 1: What Does It Really Mean?

For each idiom below, circle the correct meaning:

1. "We're barking up the wrong tree."

a) We are making too much noise in the office.

b) We are pursuing the wrong approach or looking in the wrong place.

c) We need to go outside and find a better location.

2. "Let's cut to the chase."

a) Let's move faster and make a quick decision.

b) Let's get to the main point without unnecessary preamble.

c) Let's end the meeting early.

3. "She's sitting on the fence."

a) She is comfortable with the current situation.

b) She is avoiding committing to either side of the decision.

c) She is neutral and does not need to decide.

4. "The project hit the wall."

a) The project was completed successfully.

b) The project reached a point of serious difficulty or exhaustion.

c) The project was canceled due to budget cuts.

5. "We're in hot water with the client."

a) We have a warm and productive relationship with the client.

b) We are in a difficult or troublesome situation with the client.

c) The client has requested an urgent meeting.

Exercise 2: Choose the Right Idiom

Choose the most appropriate idiom to complete each sentence:

1. "I know you want to discuss the full history of the project, but let's ______________________ and focus on the decision we need to make today." (cut to the chase / bark up the wrong tree / sit on the fence)

2. "The engineering team has been working on the wrong module all week — I think we've been ____________________." (hitting the wall / barking up the wrong tree / spilling the beans)

3. "We can't ____________________ on this pricing decision any longer — the client needs an answer by Thursday." (go back to the drawing board / sit on the fence / cut to the chase)

4. "I'm sorry — I'm a bit ____________________ today. I might need to leave the meeting early." (in hot water / under the weather / on the fence)

5. "Someone ____________________ about the new product before the press release — it's all over social media." (hit the wall / spilled the beans / cut to the chase)

Exercise 3: Asking for Clarification Professionally

Write a natural, professional response for each situation where you don't understand an idiom:

1. In a meeting, your manager says: "We need to make sure we're not throwing good money after bad on this project." You're not sure what this means. Write what you would say to clarify.

Your response: ____

2. After a presentation, a senior colleague mentions that the strategy "doesn't hold water." You want to understand what they meant. Write what you would say.

Your response: ____

3. In an email, a client writes: "We'd like to touch base before you go back to the drawing board on the proposal." Write what you would reply to confirm your understanding.

Your response: ____

Exercise 4: Your One Idiom This Week

This is a personal practice exercise with no single correct answer.

Choose one idiom from Chapters 1–6 that you haven't used yet in real conversation. Write it below along with two sentences showing how you plan to use it this week, one in writing and one in speech.

Idiom I'm practicing: ____

Sentence for writing (email or message):

____

Sentence for speaking (meeting or conversation):

____

After using it: What happened? Did it fit naturally?

____

Chapter Seven

Modern Business Vocabulary

You're in a virtual meeting when someone says: "I need to hop on a Zoom call with the dev team, make sure we're all on the same page about the timeline, and then I'll ping you with a progress update. If you have the bandwidth, could you download the latest data and give me your thoughts? I'm sharing my screen during the meeting, so having your input in my back pocket would be great."

Six modern idioms in five sentences. If you've been in any English-speaking workplace in the past decade, you've heard language like this, and if any of those expressions felt unfamiliar, you've experienced the new frontier of idiomatic English.

Technology hasn't just changed how we work. It's changed how we talk about work. This chapter covers the vocabulary that has emerged from digital transformation, remote work, the startup ecosystem, and social media, the language of the modern English-speaking professional.

7.1 Digital Transformation: Technology-Inspired Idioms

The most significant shift in business English over the past twenty years has come from technology. Terms that once lived exclusively in IT departments have migrated into everyday workplace conversation, used by people who couldn't write a line of code and wouldn't need to.

Understanding these expressions is essential not because you work in tech, but because everyone works with tech now.

Core Technology-Inspired Idioms

• In the cloud:

Meaning: stored on remote servers accessed via the internet, rather than on a local device.

Example: "All project documents are in the cloud — here's the link to the shared folder." Why it matters: used constantly in modern workplaces when discussing file storage, software, and collaboration tools.

• Plug and play:

Meaning: ready to use immediately with minimal setup required. Originally described hardware that worked when connected without additional configuration.

Example: "The new CRM system is completely plug and play — you'll be up and running within the hour." Common usage: describing any process, tool, or person that integrates smoothly without requiring extensive preparation.

• Bandwidth:

Meaning: in technology, the capacity of a network connection. In business conversation, a person's capacity to take on additional work or responsibility.

Example: "I'd love to help with the event planning, but I don't have the bandwidth this month." This is one of the most frequently used tech-to-business transfers in modern workplaces.

• Debug:

Meaning: originally, to find and fix errors in computer code. In business, to identify and solve problems in a process, strategy, or plan.

Example: "Before we launch, let's debug the onboarding flow — there are too many drop-off points." Usage note: works in both formal and informal contexts.

• Go viral:

Meaning: to spread rapidly and widely across social networks, reaching a large audience in a short time.

Example: "The campaign video went viral overnight — three million views by morning." In business: used for content, ideas, and campaigns that achieve unexpected rapid reach.

- **On my radar:**

Meaning: aware of something and monitoring it, from radar technology detecting approaching objects.

Example: "That competitor's new product launch is definitely on my radar." Usage: signals awareness and active attention without implying urgency.

- **Hard reset:**

Meaning: originally, restarting a device by cutting all power. In business, a complete restart of an approach, strategy, or process.

Example: "After two failed launches, the team needed a hard reset on the entire go-to-market strategy."

- **Beta test:**

Meaning: a trial phase where a product or process is tested by real users before full release.

Example: "We're beta testing the new portal with fifty clients before we roll it out company-wide." Usage: now used beyond technology for any limited trial before full implementation.

- **Download:**

Meaning: in its transferred business sense, to quickly brief someone on information or updates.

Example: "Let me download you on what happened in the board meeting — a lot changed." Note: distinct from its literal meaning of transferring a file.

- **Ping:**

Meaning: to send a quick message or notification to someone.

Example: "Ping me when the report is ready and I'll review it immediately." Usage: informal, used for any short digital communication, email, message, notification.

Tech Idioms in Context: Three Realistic Scenarios

Remote Work Context:

"I need to hop on a Zoom call with the development team, make sure we're all on the same page about the timeline, and then I'll ping you with a progress update. If you have the bandwidth, could you download the latest data and give me your thoughts? I'm sharing my screen during the meeting, so having your input in my back pocket would be great."

Digital Marketing Meeting:

"Our last campaign went viral on social media, but we need to debug some issues with the landing page conversions. The analytics are in the cloud if you want to look at them. Let's beta test a few different approaches before we go all in on the next campaign."

Tech Startup Pitch:

"Our solution is completely plug and play, requiring zero technical knowledge from end users. We've been flying under the radar while developing the product, but we're ready to scale up now. We've already soft-launched with fifty beta testers, and the feedback loop has been incredibly positive."

Tech Idiom Translation Challenge

Modern business emails often contain multiple tech-inspired idioms. Read the email below and write a plain-language version that removes all idioms while preserving the meaning:

Original email:

"Hi team, just a heads-up that I'm running low on bandwidth this week with the product launch. I'm trying to debug the presentation while keeping the client dashboard on my radar. Could someone download the metrics from the cloud and give me a ping when they're available? Let's also hard reset our approach to the marketing strategy since we need something that will go viral quickly. Thanks, Alex"

Write your translation before checking the Answer Key.

7.2 Navigating Virtual Meetings: Idioms for the Remote Workplace

The shift to remote and hybrid work has created its own layer of idiomatic language, expressions that either migrated from physical office settings or were born entirely in the digital workplace.

Virtual Meeting Idioms

• **Check in:**

  Meaning: a brief update or status report from team members at the start of a meeting or project milestone.

Example: "Let's do a quick check-in before we get into the agenda — how is everyone tracking on their deliverables?"

- **Circle back:**

Meaning: to return to a topic, person, or task at a later time.

Example: "I don't have the answer right now — let me circle back to you by end of day." Cultural note: overused in some workplaces to the point of becoming a cliché. Use deliberately.

- **Hop on a call:**

Meaning: to join a phone or video call, usually quickly and informally.

Example: "Can we hop on a call this afternoon? I want to walk you through the revised proposal." Formality: informal, not appropriate for senior external communications.

- **Take it offline:**

Meaning: to move a conversation out of the current meeting and continue it separately.

Example: "This is an important question but it's going to take more time than we have; let's take it offline and I'll set up a separate call."

- **You're on mute:**

Meaning: a literal instruction in virtual meetings that has become a cultural shorthand for not being heard.

In broader usage: "I felt like I was on mute throughout that discussion" means feeling ignored or unable to contribute.

- **Share my screen:**

Meaning: literally to display your screen to meeting participants.

In broader use: "Let me share my screen on this" means to show your thinking or working process transparently.

- **Async:**

Short for asynchronous. Meaning: communication or work that does not happen in real time.

Example: "Let's handle the feedback asynchronously — I'll drop comments in the document and you can respond when you have time." Increasingly common in global teams across time zones.

- **Touch base virtually:**

Meaning: to make brief contact via digital means.

Example: "Since we can't meet in person, let's touch base virtually next week." A natural evolution of "touch base" for the remote era.

The Remote Work Communication Spectrum

Understanding when to use synchronous versus asynchronous idioms matters in modern workplaces:

Synchronous: real-time communication:

"Let's hop on a call." / "Can we meet virtually this afternoon?" / "I'll share my screen so we can work through this together."

Asynchronous: communication that doesn't require immediate response:

"I'll drop my feedback in the doc." / "Let's handle this async." / "Ping me when you're ready — no rush." / "Circle back to me whenever works."

Knowing which mode fits which situation: and using the right idiom for each, signals modern professional fluency.

7.3 Staying Current: New Idioms in the Business World

Language evolves continuously. The expressions below emerged primarily in the last decade and are now standard in many professional environments. Some came from the startup world. Some from social media. Some from global events that reshaped how we work and talk about work.

Startup and Innovation Idioms

• Pivot:

Originally from basketball: turning quickly to change direction. In business: a significant strategic shift in response to new information, market feedback, or changed conditions.

Example: "After the market research came back, we made the decision to pivot from B2C to B2B entirely." Usage: one of the most widely used startup idioms, now common in all business contexts.

• Unicorn:

A startup company valued at over one billion dollars.

Example: "They achieved unicorn status three years after launch — remarkable given the market conditions." The term highlights the rarity of such success in the competitive startup ecosystem.

  • **Disrupt / Disruption:**

To fundamentally change an industry or market with a new approach, product, or business model.

Example: "This platform has the potential to disrupt the traditional real estate market." Usage note: used so frequently it risks losing meaning, use when the disruption is genuinely significant.

  • **Scale**:

To grow a business model rapidly and efficiently.

Example: "The product works beautifully at this size — the question is whether we can scale it." Also used as an adjective: "a scalable solution."

  • **Bootstrapped:**

Built and grown using only the founders' own resources, without external investment.

Example: "They bootstrapped the company for four years before seeking venture capital." Implies resourcefulness and self-reliance.

  • **Move fast and break things:**

A philosophy associated with Silicon Valley, prioritizing rapid iteration and experimentation over caution.

Example: "We've moved past the 'move fast and break things' phase — at this scale, reliability matters more than speed."

Social Media and Digital Culture Idioms

• **Influencer:** A person who shapes opinions and behavior through their social media presence. In business: "We're partnering with micro-influencers in the fitness space to reach our target demographic."

  • **Go viral:** Content that spreads rapidly across digital platforms. Already covered in 7.1, worth noting that the speed implied by "viral" is now often used hyperbolically: "This internal memo went viral within the company" means it spread quickly and unexpectedly.

  • **Hashtag**: Originally a categorization tool on social media. In business conversation: used metaphorically to label or organize ideas. "Let's hashtag this as a Q2 priority" is unusual but increasingly heard in younger professional environments.

• **Content:** In modern business, refers to any material created for communication or marketing, articles, videos, social posts, podcasts. "We need more content around our sustainability initiatives."

Post-Pandemic Workplace Idioms

• **The new normal:** The changed state of affairs after a major disruption, especially post-pandemic remote and hybrid work.

Example: "Flexible schedules have become the new normal for most knowledge workers."

• **Flatten the curve**: Originally a public health term for slowing the spread of disease. Now used in business for managing growth, resource consumption, or risk in a controlled, sustainable way.

Example: "We need to flatten the hiring curve — the onboarding team is overwhelmed."

• **Hybrid:** A work model combining in-person and remote work.

Example: "We've moved to a hybrid model — teams are in the office Tuesdays and Thursdays."

• **Quiet quitting:** Doing the minimum required by a job without formally resigning, a term that emerged to describe disengaged employees.

Example: "The survey results suggest we have a quiet quitting problem in the operations team."

• **Burnout:** Complete mental and physical exhaustion from chronic workplace stress.

Example: "After eighteen months without a real break, several senior team members are showing signs of burnout."

Chapter 7 Practice Exercises

Check your answers in the Answer Key at the back of the book.

Exercise 1: Tech Idiom Meanings

Match each tech-inspired idiom with its correct business meaning:

1. "I don't have the bandwidth for that right now." ___

2. "Let's debug the process before we go live." ___

3. "Can you download me on what happened in the meeting?" ___

4. "The campaign went viral within hours." ___

5. "All our files are in the cloud." ___

A. Stored on remote servers accessible via the internet

B. Spread rapidly to a very large audience

C. Brief me quickly on the latest information

D. I don't have the capacity to take on additional work

E. Identify and fix problems in a process or plan

Exercise 2: Virtual Meeting Vocabulary

Choose the correct idiom to complete each virtual meeting sentence:

1. "The discussion about the rebrand is going to take more time than we have today — let's _________________ and schedule a separate session." (take it offline / circle back / hop on a call)

2. "Could you _________________ this afternoon? I want to walk you through the updated timeline." (share your screen / hop on a call / check in)

3. "Before we get into the agenda, let's do a quick _________________ — how is everyone tracking on their deliverables?" (ping / check-in / hard reset)

4. "I'll drop the feedback in the document — we can handle the revisions _________________." (on my radar / async / in the cloud)

5. "Can you _________________ so we can see the dashboard you're referring to?" (ping me / share your screen / go viral)

Exercise 3: Old World or New World?

Each idiom below is either a traditional business idiom or a modern tech-era expression. Label each T (traditional, pre-2000) or M (modern, emerged primarily post-2000):

1. "Let's table the discussion." ___

2. "The startup decided to pivot." ___

3. "She doesn't have the bandwidth." ___

4. "Get the ball rolling." ___

5. "They achieved unicorn status." ___

6. "The bottom line is this." ___

7. "We need to debug the strategy." ___

8. "Let's circle back on this." ___

Exercise 4: Tech Idiom Translation

Translate the following tech-heavy email into plain language that would be understood by someone unfamiliar with these idioms. Remove all modern idioms and replace them with their plain-language equivalents.

Original:

"Hi team, just a heads-up that I'm running low on bandwidth this week with the product launch. I'm trying to debug the presentation while keeping the client dashboard on my radar. Could someone download the metrics from the cloud and give me a ping when they're available? Let's also hard reset our approach to the marketing strategy since we need something that will go viral quickly. Thanks, Alex"

Your translation:

____

____

____

Exercise 5: Emerging Vocabulary Check

For each modern idiom below, write a sentence using it correctly in a professional context:

1. Pivot:

____

2. The new normal:

____

3. Scale:

____

4. Async:

____

Interactive Learning Strategies

You've read the explanations. You've studied the examples. You understand what "iron out the details" means and you know "touch base" signals a brief check-in. But the next morning in a real meeting, when the moment arrives to use one of these expressions naturally, something stops you.

This is the gap between passive knowledge and active fluency, and it's closed by only one thing: deliberate practice in conditions that resemble real use.

This chapter is your practical toolkit. Not theory about how to learn idioms, but specific, structured activities you can do today, this week, and every week going forward, until the expressions you've studied become the expressions you reach for without thinking.

8.1 Building Your Practice Routine

The single most important insight about learning idiomatic language is this: reading about idioms does not make you fluent in idioms. Using them does. And using them in low-stakes practice environments is what makes high-stakes real-world use feel natural rather than terrifying.

Here is a four-part weekly practice routine that works regardless of your current level.

Part 1: Daily Idiom Journal (10 minutes per day)

Each day, work through this sequence for one idiom:

Day 1: Choose and define: Select one idiom from your current chapter. Write it down with its meaning, its formality level, and the contexts where it fits.

Day 2: Contextualize it: Write two sentences using the idiom, one from your actual work context, one from a different professional scenario.

Day 3: Use it in writing: Send an email, message, or document today that includes this idiom naturally. It doesn't need to be prominent, it just needs to be there.

Day 4: Use it in speech: Find one opportunity in a meeting, a call, or a casual conversation to use the expression.

Day 5: Reflect: Did it land naturally? Did anyone react? Would you use it again in the same way? Write three sentences about what you noticed.

Weekend: Review: Look back at the week's entry. Is this expression now yours? Or does it need another week?

Part 2: Flashcard System

Create a flashcard for every idiom you want to own, not just the ones you've studied. Physical flashcards work well. Digital tools like Anki work even better because they use spaced repetition, showing you cards at increasing intervals as you learn them.

Each flashcard should have:

• Front: the idiom in a sentence with the idiom blanked out

• Back: the idiom, its meaning, and its formality level

Review your deck for five minutes each morning. The goal is not to memorize, it's to make retrieval automatic.

Part 3: Weekly Role-Play Session

Once a week, practice at least one role-play scenario from the list in section 8.2 below, alone, with a language partner, or with a colleague who is also developing their English.

Part 4: Progress Check

At the end of each month, take the self-assessment quiz in section 8.3. Track your scores. Watching your own progress is one of the most powerful motivators in language learning.

8.2 Role-Playing Scenarios: Real-World Practice

Role-play is the most effective preparation for real idiomatic fluency because it forces you to produce language under mild pressure, which is exactly the condition real conversations create.

The scenarios below are ready to use. For each one, your goal is to use at least four idioms naturally within the conversation. The suggested idioms are listed, but if you can use others from earlier chapters, even better.

Scenario 1: The Project Kickoff Meeting

Setting: You are the project lead opening a kickoff meeting for a new client initiative. Four team members are present. The client will join for the last fifteen minutes.

Your role: Open the meeting, set expectations, invite participation, and prepare the team for the client's arrival.

Suggested idioms to use: kick things off / set the stage / get the ball rolling / on the same page / open the floor

Opening line to get you started:

"Thanks everyone for being here. Let's kick things off — I want to set the stage before the client joins us at the end of the hour..."

After the role-play, reflect on:

- Which idioms did you use naturally and which felt forced?
- Did the conversation flow? Where did it stall?
- What would you do differently?

Scenario 2: The Difficult Negotiation

Setting: You are negotiating revised contract terms with a supplier who wants a higher price than your budget allows. You need to reach a compromise without damaging the relationship.

Your role: Negotiate professionally, acknowledge their position, and work toward a resolution.

Suggested idioms to use: meet halfway / find common ground / drive a hard bargain / back down / seal the deal / agree to disagree

Opening line to get you started:

"I appreciate you making time for this conversation. I want to find common ground here — I think there's a deal to be made, but I need to be honest about what our budget allows..."

After the role-play, reflect on:

• Did you maintain a professional tone while holding your position?

• Which idioms helped the negotiation feel natural?

• What would you change?

Scenario 3: The Performance Review

Setting: You are a manager conducting a quarterly performance review with a team member. The review includes both praise and constructive feedback. The conversation needs to be honest but supportive.

Your role: Open the review, acknowledge strengths, address areas for improvement, and close with clear next steps.

Suggested idioms to use: hit the ground running / raise the bar / back to the drawing board / step up to the plate / move forward / plant a seed

Opening line to get you started:

"Thanks for coming in. I want to start by saying you really hit the ground running this quarter — the client feedback has been excellent. I also want to talk about a couple of areas where I think we can raise the bar together..."

After the role-play, reflect on:

• Did the idioms make the feedback feel more natural or more stiff?

• Which expressions were hardest to use in this context?

Scenario 4: The Virtual Team Meeting

Setting: You are facilitating a virtual team meeting with five participants across three time zones. The agenda includes a project update, a problem that needs solving, and a decision that needs to be made before the end of the call.

Your role: Keep the meeting on track, invite participation, handle a derailing discussion, and close with clear actions.

Suggested idioms to use: touch base / circle back / take it offline / on the same page / chime in / move forward / hop on a call

Opening line to get you started:

"Good morning, good afternoon, good evening depending on where you are — thanks for joining. Let's touch base quickly on where everyone stands before we get into the main agenda..."

Scenario 5: The Networking Conversation

Setting: You are at an industry conference. You've just introduced yourself to someone whose work you've followed for a while. The conversation is going well and you want to establish a genuine professional connection.

Your role: Build rapport, express genuine interest, and close with a clear next step.

Suggested idioms to use: break the ice / hit it off / pick your brain / reach out / follow up / keep in touch

Opening line to get you started:

"I have to say, I've been following your work on supply chain innovation for about a year now — your Q3 case study was genuinely impressive. I'm glad we finally got to break the ice in person..."

8.3 Quizzes and Reflections: Assessing Your Progress

Monthly Self-Assessment Quiz

Use this quiz at the end of each month to measure your progress. Answer without looking back at the chapters, the point is to test genuine recall.

Section A: Multiple Choice

For each sentence, choose the idiom that best completes it:

1. "The project has stalled and we're back to ________________."

a) hitting the ground running

b) the drawing board

c) the same page

2. "I don't have the _________________ to take on another project this month."

a) bottom line

b) bandwidth

c) ballpark

3. "Let's ________________ this discussion and schedule a separate call."

a) take offline

b) circle back

c) open the floor

4. "She really _________________ in the first week — the team was impressed."

a) hit it off

b) hit the ground running

c) hit the nail on the head

5. "Before we close, let's make sure we're all _________________."

a) in the loop

b) on the same page

c) on the fence

Section B: True or False

Write T (true) or F (false) for each statement:

1. "Table the discussion" means the same thing in American and British English. ___

2. "Bite the bullet" means to make a quick decision. ___

3. "Beta test" originally came from software development. ___

4. "Pick someone's brain" means to ask for someone's informal expertise. ___

5. Sports-based idioms are generally safe to use with all international audiences. ___

Section C: Fill in the Blank

Complete each sentence with the correct idiom:

1. "We can't keep avoiding this decision — we need to _________________ and commit." (bite the bullet / bark up the wrong tree / burn the midnight oil)

2. "The team worked all weekend — they really _________________ to finish before the deadline." (burned the midnight oil / hit the wall / went viral)

3. "I'll _________________ once I've spoken to the legal team and have a clearer picture." (circle back / take it offline / loop in)

Reflection Questions

After each practice session or at the end of each week, work through these reflection questions in your journal:

1. Which idiom from this week's study do I feel most confident using? Why?

2. Which expression am I still uncertain about? What specifically confuses me?

3. Did I use any idiom from this book in a real conversation this week? What happened?

4. What's one situation that came up this week where an idiom from this book would have been useful, but I didn't use it?

5. What is my focus for next week?

Chapter 8 Practice Exercises

Check your answers in the Answer Key at the back of the book.

Exercise 1: Monthly Quiz: Section A

(Use the Multiple Choice questions from section 8.3 above)

Exercise 2: Monthly Quiz: Section B

(Use the True or False questions from section 8.3 above)

Exercise 3: Monthly Quiz: Section C

(Use the Fill in the Blank questions from section 8.3 above)

Exercise 4: Design Your Own Role-Play

Create a role-play scenario from your own professional context. Write:

1. The setting (where, who is involved, what the situation is):

____

2. Your role and goal in the conversation:

____

3. At least five idioms from this book you plan to use:

- ____

- ____

- ____

- ____

- ____

4. Your opening line to start the role-play:

____

Exercise 5: Your 30-Day Idiom Learning Plan

Map out your next 30 days of idiom practice. For each week, write:

Week 1: Idiom focus (which chapter or topic): _______________

Goal for the week: _______________

How you will practice (writing / speaking / role-play): _______________

Week 2: Idiom focus: _______________

Goal for the week: _______________

How you will practice: _______________

Week 3: Idiom focus: _______________

Goal for the week: _______________

How you will practice: _______________

Week 4: Idiom focus: _______________

Goal for the week: _______________

How you will practice: _______________

Chapter Nine

Idioms for Team Collaboration

I t's 4:45 PM on a Friday. The product launch is Monday. Something has gone wrong with the integration, and your team leader appears in the doorway and says: "All hands on deck — we need to rally the troops and get this across the finish line before the weekend."

Three idioms. One sentence. And every person in that room knows exactly what is required of them.

This is what team idioms do that plain language cannot, they compress urgency, unity, and shared purpose into a few words that land instantly. "All hands on deck" doesn't just mean everyone should help. It carries the weight of a ship in crisis, of collective survival, of no one sitting on the sidelines. That weight is what motivates people.

This chapter covers the idiomatic language of teamwork, building unity, navigating conflict, and celebrating the wins that keep a team going.

9.1 Building Team Unity: Idioms for Collaboration

The most effective team idioms do two things simultaneously: they communicate information and they reinforce culture. When a leader says "we're in the same boat," they're not just describing a shared situation, they're reminding everyone that they rise and fall together.

Core Team Collaboration Idioms

- **All hands on deck:**

    Meaning: everyone must contribute, all resources are needed.

    Origin: nautical, every sailor required during a crisis at sea.

    Example: "The server went down at the worst possible moment — it's all hands on deck until we're back online." Usage: conveys urgency and collective responsibility. Use when a genuine crisis or major deadline requires full team mobilization.

    - **In the same boat:**

    Meaning: facing the same challenges or circumstances together.

    Example: "I know the new reporting requirements are frustrating — we're all in the same boat on this one." Usage: builds solidarity, particularly useful when addressing shared difficulties or unpopular changes.

    - **Pull together:**

    Meaning: to work as a unified team toward a common goal.

    Example: "This has been a difficult quarter, but I've seen this team pull together before and I know we'll do it again." Usage: motivational, best used in team addresses or difficult moments.

    - **Carry the team:**

    Meaning:

    to do a disproportionate share of the work, keeping the team afloat.

    Example: "She carried the team through the product launch — without her, we would have missed the deadline entirely." Usage: acknowledgment of exceptional individual contribution within a team context.

    - **Pick up the slack:**

    Meaning: to do extra work to compensate when a team member is unable to contribute fully.

    Example: "With three people out sick, the rest of the team really stepped up to pick up the slack." Usage: signals appreciation for flexibility and extra effort.

    - **On the same page:**

    Meaning: sharing the same understanding, aligned.

Example: "Before we assign tasks, I want to make sure we're all on the same page about what success looks like for this project." Usage: one of the most frequently used team idioms, versatile across all contexts.

• **Pass the baton:**

Meaning: to hand responsibility to the next person in a sequence, from relay racing.

Example: "I'm passing the baton to Kenji for the client relationship — he'll be your main point of contact going forward." Usage: transitions of responsibility, handovers, succession.

• **Get buy-in:**

Meaning: to gain agreement and commitment from stakeholders or team members before proceeding.

Example: "Before we finalize the strategy, we need to get buy-in from the regional directors." Usage: critical in any decision that requires others' cooperation to implement.

• **Rally the troops:**

Meaning: to motivate and energize the team before a challenge.

Example: "Before the big pitch, the sales director rallied the troops with a reminder of how far we'd come." Usage: leadership contexts, team addresses before important moments.

• **Across the finish line:**

Meaning: to complete something successfully, especially after difficulty.

Example: "We've done the hard work — now let's get this project across the finish line." Usage: motivational, used near the end of a project or challenge.

Team Idioms in Natural Flow

The following dialogue shows how these idioms appear in a realistic team conversation:

Team leader: "Okay everyone, I know we're exhausted, but we need all hands on deck for the next forty-eight hours. We're in the same boat here — if the launch fails, it affects all of us."

Team member: "What do you need from us?"

Team leader: "First, I need to make sure we're all on the same page on the revised timeline. Then I need Sarah's team to pick up the slack on the documentation while the engineers focus on the fix. Once we get buy-in from the client on the revised scope, we can rally the troops for the final push and get this thing across the finish line."

9.2 Handling Conflicts: Idioms for Diplomacy

Conflict in professional settings is inevitable. The question is not whether disagreements will arise but whether the language used to navigate them will move things toward resolution or make them worse.

The idioms below are your diplomatic toolkit, expressions that acknowledge tension, invite dialogue, and create the conditions for genuine resolution without anyone losing face.

Conflict Navigation Idioms

- **Bury the hatchet:**

    Meaning: to resolve a dispute and move forward, letting go of past grievances.

    Origin: from a Native American peace ritual of literally burying weapons.

    Example: "The two departments have been in conflict for months — it's time to bury the hatchet and focus on the shared goal." Usage note: appropriate when both parties are ready to move forward. Using it too early can feel dismissive.

    - **Clear the air:**

    Meaning: to openly address misunderstandings or tensions so they no longer affect the relationship or work.

    Example: "I think we need to clear the air about what happened in last week's meeting before we can move forward productively." Usage: signals willingness to have a direct but constructive conversation.

    - **Extend an olive branch:**

    Meaning: to make a gesture of goodwill or reconciliation, especially after conflict. Origin: the olive branch as a symbol of peace.

    Example: "After the difficult exchange on the call, I'm going to extend an olive branch and propose a fresh start." Usage: formal enough for serious professional contexts, signals genuine intention to resolve.

    - **Find common ground:**

    Meaning: to identify shared interests or goals as a basis for agreement.

Example: "We may not agree on the approach, but I think we can find common ground on the outcome we're both trying to achieve." Usage: one of the most useful conflict resolution idioms, redirects from positions to interests.

• Let bygones be bygones:

Meaning: to forgive past mistakes or conflicts and not allow them to affect the present.

Example: "There were mistakes on both sides last quarter — I think we should let bygones be bygones and focus on Q3." Usage: signals generosity and forward focus. Best when both parties have acknowledged the issue.

• Keep a lid on it:

Meaning: to prevent emotions or a situation from escalating.

Example: "I know you're frustrated with the decision, but I need you to keep a lid on it until we've had a chance to discuss it privately." Usage: direct but respectful, works when addressing someone whose reaction risks affecting the team.

• Smooth things over:

Meaning: to make a tense situation calmer, often through diplomacy or small concessions.

Example: "After the difficult review, the manager took the client to lunch to smooth things over." Usage: informal, signals relationship repair through gesture rather than formal process.

• Come to the table:

Meaning: to be willing to negotiate or discuss, to participate constructively in resolution.

Example: "Both sides need to come to the table with a willingness to compromise — otherwise this goes nowhere." Usage: signals expectation of good-faith participation.

Conflict Resolution in Practice: A Three-Stage Model

Stage 1: Acknowledge the tension:

"I think we need to clear the air about what happened last week. There's clearly some tension here and I'd rather address it directly than let it affect our work."

Stage 2: Find shared ground:

"I know we see this differently, but I think we can find common ground on what we're both ultimately trying to achieve for the client."

Stage 3: Move toward resolution:

"I'd like to extend an olive branch here — I think if we both come to the table with a little flexibility, we can resolve this and let bygones be bygones."

Notice how each stage uses a different idiom that fits the emotional moment precisely. Stage 1 requires honesty. Stage 2 requires redirection. Stage 3 requires generosity. The right idiom at the right moment is what makes the difference.

9.3 Celebrating Success: Idioms for Acknowledging Achievements

Recognition matters. Studies consistently show that feeling acknowledged and appreciated is one of the strongest predictors of employee engagement and retention. And the language of recognition, how you celebrate wins, acknowledge effort, and encourage future performance, is where idioms do some of their most powerful work.

Recognition and Celebration Idioms

• **Pat on the back:**

Meaning: an expression of praise and recognition for a job well done.

Example: "I want to give the entire project team a pat on the back — you delivered under incredibly difficult conditions." Usage: warm and informal, works in team emails, meetings, and casual acknowledgment.

• **Job well done:**

Meaning: direct, sincere recognition of quality work.

Example: "That presentation was exactly what the client needed — job well done." Usage: simple but effective, sometimes the most direct expression carries the most weight.

• **Raise the bar:**

Meaning: to set a higher standard, to perform at a level that becomes the new benchmark.

Example: "This quarter's results didn't just meet expectations — they raised the bar for what this team is capable of." Usage: forward-looking praise that acknowledges current achievement while inspiring future performance.

• **Hit it out of the park:**

Meaning: to perform exceptionally well, to far exceed expectations.

Origin: baseball, hitting the ball so hard it leaves the stadium.

Example: "The marketing campaign hit it out of the park — engagement was three times our forecast." Usage note: baseball origin, use with care in international contexts. May need paraphrasing for non-American audiences.

- **Go the extra mile:**

Meaning: to do more than is required or expected.

Example: "Yuna went the extra mile on the client report — the additional analysis she included made a real difference." Usage: one of the most universally understood recognition idioms, appropriate in all contexts.

- **Keep up the good work:**

Meaning: ongoing encouragement to maintain current high performance.

Example: "The feedback from the client has been outstanding — keep up the good work." Usage: continuous encouragement rather than one-time recognition.

- **On top of the world:**

Meaning: feeling great pride and elation after a success.

Example: "When the deal closed, the whole team was on top of the world." Usage: describes feeling rather than performance, good for capturing team emotional high after a win.

- **Celebrate the wins:**

Meaning: to take time to acknowledge and enjoy achievements, even small ones.

Example: "I know we're already thinking about Q4, but let's take a moment to celebrate the wins from this quarter." Usage: leadership reminder that recognition matters alongside the drive for continuous improvement.

Recognition in Different Contexts

In a team meeting:

"Before we get into the agenda, I want to take a moment to give the implementation team a real pat on the back. You went the extra mile under impossible conditions and hit it out of the park. That raised the bar for the entire organization — and I mean that."

In a written message:

"Just a quick note to say - job well done on the proposal. The level of detail and the quality of the analysis were exceptional. Keep up the good work, and let's celebrate the win properly at the team lunch on Friday."

In a one-on-one review:

"I want to make sure you know that your contributions this quarter didn't go unnoticed. You raised the bar in terms of what we expect from client communication. I hope you're feeling on top of the world - you should be."

Chapter 9 Practice Exercises

Check your answers in the Answer Key at the back of the book.

Exercise 1 – Team Idiom Identification

For each sentence, identify which team context the idiom fits best, Unity (U), Conflict Resolution (CR), or Recognition (R):

1. "Let's bury the hatchet and focus on delivering for the client." ___
2. "It's all hands on deck until the system is back online." ___
3. "She went the extra mile and the client noticed." ___
4. "We need to find common ground before this affects the whole team." ___
5. "Let's make sure we're all on the same page before we split into workstreams." ___
6. "That pitch hit it out of the park — job well done." ___
7. "I'd like to extend an olive branch and propose we start fresh." ___
8. "Pass the baton to Marcus once the discovery phase is complete." ___

Exercise 2 - Choose the Right Idiom

Select the most appropriate idiom to complete each sentence:

1. "Before we finalize the plan, we need to __________________ from all department heads — otherwise implementation will be a battle." (get buy-in / bury the hatchet / raise the bar)
2. "There's clearly some tension from last week's meeting. Can we find time to __________________ before Thursday's call?" (clear the air / pass the baton / go the extra mile)

3. "I know it's been a difficult quarter, but I've seen this team ___________________ before and I know we'll do it again." (carry the team / pull together / keep a lid on it)

4. "Both teams need to ___________________ with a genuine willingness to compromise — this can't be resolved any other way." (come to the table / let bygones be bygones / smooth things over)

5. "That campaign ___________________ — the results exceeded every benchmark we set." (raised the bar / hit it out of the park / cleared the air)

Exercise 3 - Conflict Resolution Script

You are a team leader. Two of your team members, Amara and David, have been in conflict over ownership of a project deliverable for two weeks. The tension is affecting the rest of the team. You need to bring them together for a conversation.

Write a short opening statement (5–8 sentences) using at least four idioms from section 9.2. Your statement should:

- Acknowledge the tension without taking sides
- Signal your intention to resolve it
- Invite both parties to participate constructively
- End with a forward-looking statement

Your opening statement:

____

____

____

Exercise 4: Recognition Messages

Write a short recognition message for each scenario below, using at least two idioms from section 9.3 in each:

1. A team member stayed late for three nights to fix a critical bug before a major client demonstration.

Your message:

____

2. Your entire team delivered a project two weeks ahead of schedule despite losing a key member mid-project.

Your message:

____

3. A colleague gave a presentation that won a new client worth significantly more than expected.

Your message:

____

Exercise 5: Cultural Adaptation

Three idioms from this chapter require careful handling in international contexts. For each one below, write an alternative expression that conveys the same meaning but is more universally understood:

1. "Hit it out of the park" (baseball reference, may confuse non-American audiences)

Your alternative:

____

2. "Bury the hatchet" (cultural origin may be unfamiliar)

Your alternative:

____

3. "Rally the troops" (military reference, may feel aggressive in some cultures)

Your alternative:

____

Chapter Ten

Enhancing Written Communication

Written English is where many non-native speakers feel most exposed. In a conversation, you have the context of tone, facial expression, and body language to help fill gaps. In writing, the words stand alone. An email that reads as too casual can undermine a professional relationship. A report that feels flat can bury important insights. A formal letter that misses the right register can cost you credibility before a conversation even begins.

Idioms in written communication serve a specific purpose: they compress complex ideas into compact expressions, add warmth or authority depending on context, and signal fluency in a way that plain language does not. The challenge is knowing which idioms belong where, and which ones would be completely out of place.

This chapter covers three core written contexts: emails, reports, and formal correspondence, with specific idioms for each, before-and-after examples, and guidance on formality and appropriateness.

10.1 Crafting Persuasive Emails: Idioms That Move People to Act

Email is the dominant form of professional written communication. The average professional receives over a hundred emails per day, which means your message is competing for attention, and every word either earns or loses that attention.

Idioms in emails do two things: they make the writing feel human rather than robotic, and they signal intent clearly without requiring long explanations.

Email Idioms by Purpose

Opening and relationship-building:

- **Break the ice:**

Signal warmth and approachability in a first outreach.

Example: "I wanted to break the ice with a quick note about the opportunity we discussed at last week's event."

- **Put your best foot forward:**

Signal commitment and quality at the start of a new relationship.

Example: "We want to put our best foot forward on this proposal — please find our full capabilities overview attached."

- **Get the ball rolling**:

Initiate action or begin a project.

Example: "I'd love to get the ball rolling on the partnership, are you available for a call this week?"

Clarifying and directing:

- Cut to the chase:

Signal that you are getting directly to the key point.

Example: "I'll cut to the chase, we need a decision on the pricing by Thursday to hold the delivery slot."

- **Leave no stone unturned:**

Signal thoroughness and comprehensive effort.

Example: "We've left no stone unturned in preparing this proposal; I'm confident it addresses every concern you raised."

- **Put all your cards on the table:**

Signal full transparency and honest disclosure.

Example: "I'd like to put all our cards on the table so we can make a decision that works for both sides."

Closing and moving to action:

- **Seal the deal:**

Signal readiness to finalize and commit.

Example: "I believe we have everything we need to seal the deal; shall I send over the contract?"

• Move forward:

Signal transition from discussion to action.

Example: "I'm ready to move forward whenever you are; please let me know your preferred next step."

• Touch base:

Signal a follow-up or check-in intention.

Example: "I'll touch base with you next week to see how the onboarding is going."

Before and After: The Difference Idioms Make in Email

Before: plain language, functional but flat:

Subject: Following up on our discussion

Hi Maria,

I am following up on our conversation from last week. I would like to schedule a call to discuss the proposal. Please let me know when you are available. I want to make sure we address all your questions before you make a decision.

Best regards,

James

After: same message, idioms added strategically:

Subject: Following up: ready to move forward

Hi Maria,

I wanted to touch base after our conversation last week, I hope you've had a chance to review the proposal. I'll cut to the chase: we're excited about this opportunity and want to put our best foot forward as your partner.

I'd love to get the ball rolling on a follow-up call this week. I'm happy to put all our cards on the table and address any remaining questions before you make your decision.

Looking forward to hearing from you.

James

What changed: The second email is warmer, more direct, and signals genuine engagement. The idioms don't add length, they replace flat phrases with expressions that carry more weight and personality.

Appropriate vs. Inappropriate Email Idioms

Not every idiom belongs in every email. Formality level and recipient relationship determine what fits.

Formal email to a new senior client: appropriate idioms:

- **"Put our best foot forward"**, professional, signals commitment
- **"Leave no stone unturned"**, thorough, appropriate for high-stakes contexts
- **"In light of the above"**, formal connective, excellent for proposals and reports

Formal email to a new senior client: inappropriate idioms:

- **"Shoot me an email"**, too casual
- **"Pick your brain"**, too informal for first senior contact
- **"Touch base"**, borderline, acceptable in some corporate cultures, too casual in others

Informal email to a trusted colleague: appropriate idioms:

- "Touch base," "circle back," "get the ball rolling," "hop on a call"

Informal email to a trusted colleague: avoid:

- Legal-sounding formal language that creates unnecessary distance

10.2 Writing Reports with Flair: Incorporating Idioms

Reports are the most common place where non-native English speakers under-use idioms, defaulting to purely technical language that is accurate but difficult to engage with. A well-placed idiom in a report does not make it less professional. It makes complex data more accessible and the argument more memorable.

The key is context-appropriateness: the right idiom in the right section.

Report

Idioms by Section

Executive summary: idioms that are appropriate:

- **"The big picture"**, to frame the overall situation.
  Example: "The big picture shows consistent growth in three of our four markets."
- **"Key takeaways"**, to signal the most important points.
  Example: "The key takeaways from this quarter's data are as follows."

- **"Breaking new ground"**, to highlight innovation or first-time results.

Example: "Our digital channel is breaking new ground, outperforming traditional sales for the first time."

Report body: idioms that are appropriate:

- **"Connect the dots"**, to show how separate data points relate.

Example: "To connect the dots between these findings: the drop in engagement directly precedes the decline in conversion."

- **"Paint a picture"**, to make data visual and concrete.

Example: "The customer satisfaction data paints a picture of a market that is more price-sensitive than we anticipated."

- **"Drill down"**, to examine details below the surface.

Example: "Drilling down into the regional data reveals a significant variance between the North and South territories."

- **"Hit the nail on the head"**, to confirm a precise finding.

Example: "The research hits the nail on the head: speed of response is the single most important driver of client retention."

Risk and challenge sections: idioms that are appropriate:

- **"Red flags"**, to signal warning signs.

Example: "The Q3 audit revealed several red flags in the expense reporting process that require immediate attention."

- **"Leave no stone unturned"**, to signal thorough investigation.

Example: "We have left no stone unturned in reviewing the compliance documentation."

- **"Get to the bottom of"**, to signal investigation intent.

Example: "We are committed to getting to the bottom of the discrepancy in the sales figures."

Report conclusion: idioms that are appropriate:

- **"The bottom line"**, to state the essential conclusion.

Example: "The bottom line: revenue is up, costs are down, and the business is well-positioned for Q4."

- **"Tie up loose ends"**, to signal comprehensive coverage.

Example: "This final section ties up loose ends from the earlier analysis."

- **"Bring it all together"**, to signal synthesis.

Example: "To bring it all together: the three initiatives outlined here represent the clearest path to sustainable growth."

Before and After: Report Language Transformed

Before: without idioms:

The quarterly sales data indicates a decrease in the Western region, with a 12% reduction compared to last quarter. The Eastern region shows an increase of 8%. The data suggests that the new marketing campaign has been more effective in some geographical areas than others. Additional analysis is needed to understand the regional differences.

After: with strategic idioms:

The quarterly sales data paints a picture of contrasting regional performance. While the Western region has experienced a 12% decrease, the Eastern region is bucking the trend with an 8% increase. These numbers speak volumes about the varying impact of our new marketing campaign across different geographies. To get to the bottom of these regional differences, we need to drill down into the data and connect the dots between our marketing spend and customer response patterns.

What changed: The revised version uses six idioms, "paints a picture," "bucking the trend," "speak volumes," "get to the bottom of," "drill down," "connect the dots", to transform static data into an active narrative. The facts are identical. The readability is significantly higher.

Report

Idioms to Avoid

Some idioms are inappropriate in formal reports regardless of context:

- **"Shoot from the hip"**, too casual, implies lack of preparation
- **"Ball is in your court"**, too conversational for a written report
- **"Between a rock and a hard place"**, too colloquial for formal analysis
- **"Back to square one"**, signals failure too bluntly in a professional document
- **"Piece of cake"**, undermines the seriousness of the subject matter

10.3 Enhancing Professional Correspondence: Idioms in Formal Writing

Formal correspondence: business letters, official proposals, regulatory submissions, and senior-level communications, requires a different register from everyday emails. The idioms appropriate here tend to be more established, more restrained, and carry institutional weight rather than personal warmth.

Formal Correspondence Idioms

• **In light of:** To provide context or justification. Example: "In light of the recent regulatory changes, we have revised our compliance framework accordingly."

• **At your earliest convenience:** A polite but clear request for timely action.

Example: "We would appreciate your response at your earliest convenience." Usage note: do not use when the matter is genuinely urgent, the phrase softens urgency, which can be a problem.

• **Please find attached / enclosed:** Standard formal opener for directing attention to documents.

Example: "Please find attached our updated proposal for your review."

• **We would be grateful:** Formal expression of appreciation and request. Example: "We would be grateful for the opportunity to present our findings in person."

• **We are committed to:** Strong statement of intent and reliability. Example: "We are committed to delivering the highest standard of service throughout the duration of this contract."

• **In due course:** Indicating future action without specifying exact timing. Example: "The committee will review all submissions and respond in due course." Usage note: avoid when a specific deadline is expected, this phrase delays without committing.

• **With reference to:** Formal way to connect correspondence to previous communications. Example: "With reference to your letter of March 12th, we write to confirm the arrangements discussed."

• **For your consideration:** Formal phrase for submitting something for review or approval. Example: "We submit this proposal for your consideration and look forward to your feedback."

Formality Spectrum: Written Communication

Highly formal: legal documents, regulatory submissions, board communications:

"With reference to," "In light of," "For your consideration," "We are committed to," "Please find enclosed"

Formal: business proposals, client letters, senior communications:

"At your earliest convenience," "We would be grateful," "In due course," "Please find attached"

Neutral: standard professional emails, internal reports, team communications:

"Touch base," "Get the ball rolling," "On the same page," "The bottom line," "Move forward"

Informal: colleague emails, instant messages, casual professional exchanges:

"Hop on a call," "Circle back," "Ping me," "Shoot me an email," "Loop in"

Chapter 10 Practice Exercises

Check your answers in the Answer Key at the back of the book.

Exercise 1: Email Idiom Selection

For each email context below, choose the most appropriate idiom from the options provided:

1. You are writing a first email to a new potential client you met at a conference. You want to open warmly and suggest a follow-up call.

Best idiom to use: (break the ice / drill down / leave no stone unturned)

2. You are following up on a proposal and want to signal you are ready to finalize if they are.

Best idiom to use: (get the ball rolling / seal the deal / touch base)

3. You want to get directly to your key request without lengthy preamble.

Best idiom to use: (cut to the chase / put your best foot forward / connect the dots)

4. You want to signal complete transparency before a difficult negotiation.

Best idiom to use: (put all your cards on the table / move forward / the bottom line)

5. You are closing an email and want to indicate you will check in soon.

Best idiom to use: (seal the deal / touch base / break the ice)

Exercise 2: Report Language Transformation

Take the following plain-language paragraph from a project status report and rewrite it using at least four appropriate idioms from section 10.2. Maintain the professional tone of a formal report.

Original:

"The project is currently delayed by approximately two weeks due to supply chain issues. The vendor has informed us of production delays. We are considering alternative suppliers to address the situation. The budget remains within acceptable parameters despite these challenges."

Your rewritten version:

____

____

____

Exercise 3: Appropriate or Inappropriate?

For each idiom below, decide whether it is Appropriate (A) or Inappropriate (I) for the context specified:

1. Using "shoot me an email" in a formal letter to a new client. ____
2. Using "the bottom line" in an executive summary. ____
3. Using "piece of cake" in a risk assessment report. ____
4. Using "in light of" in a formal regulatory submission. ____
5. Using "get the ball rolling" in an email to a trusted colleague. ____
6. Using "back to square one" in a formal board report. ____

Exercise 4: Formal vs. Informal Sorting

Sort the following idioms into the correct column, Formal Written English or Informal Written English:

Idioms: "in due course" / "hop on a call" / "with reference to" / "ping me" / "please find attached" / "circle back" / "for your consideration" / "shoot me an email"

Formal Written English:

____

Informal Written English:

____

Exercise 5: Write a Professional Email

You need to follow up with a senior client after a proposal meeting last week. The meeting went well but they haven't responded yet. Write a short professional email (6–8 sentences) that:

- Opens with a warm reference to the meeting
- Gets directly to your key message
- Signals your readiness to move forward
- Closes with a clear and polite next step

Use at least four idioms from this chapter, chosen for the appropriate formality level of a senior client relationship.

Your email:

____

____

____

Chapter Eleven

Idioms for Negotiation and Persuasion

Every negotiation is a conversation about value, and the language used to navigate that conversation determines as much as the numbers themselves. When a seasoned negotiator says "I want to make sure we cover all our bases before we get to the table," they're not just being thorough. They're signaling preparation, professionalism, and respect for the process. When they say "let's make this a win-win," they're reframing the conversation from competition to collaboration before a single concession has been made.

For non-native speakers, negotiation settings are among the most challenging idiomatic environments, high stakes, fast-moving, and filled with sports metaphors, strategic language, and subtle signals that native speakers read automatically. This chapter gives you the complete negotiation idiom toolkit: preparation, persuasion, and handling resistance.

11.1 Preparing to Negotiate: Strategic Idioms

Preparation is where negotiations are won or lost, long before anyone sits at the table. The idioms below are the language of strategic readiness. They appear in pre-negotiation briefings, internal strategy sessions, and the mindset conversations that happen before the real conversation begins.

Preparation Idioms

• **Cover all the bases:**

Meaning: to prepare thoroughly by addressing every possible angle or concern.

Origin: baseball, a fielder covering each base to prevent the opposing team from scoring.

Example: "Before we go into this meeting, let's make sure we've covered all the bases — pricing, timeline, and delivery terms." Usage: signals thoroughness and professional diligence.

• **Get your ducks in a row:**

Meaning: to organize everything carefully and ensure all elements are properly arranged before proceeding.

Example: "I want to get our ducks in a row before the client call — can we run through the key points one more time?" Usage: informal to neutral, appropriate for internal preparation discussions.

• **Have a plan B:**

Meaning: to prepare an alternative course of action in case the primary strategy fails.

Example: "We need to go in with a plan B on the pricing — if they push back on the rate, we need to be ready to counter with the phased payment option." Usage: universal, appropriate in all negotiation contexts.

• **Roll with the punches:**

Meaning: to remain flexible and adapt to unexpected developments without losing composure. Origin: boxing, moving with the force of a punch to reduce its impact.

Example: "In negotiation, things rarely go exactly as planned; you need to be able to roll with the punches and adjust in real time." Usage: describes mindset and adaptability.

• **Bring your A-game:**

Meaning: to perform at your highest level, to show up fully prepared and engaged.

Example: "This is our biggest client; everyone needs to bring their A-game to Thursday's negotiation."

Usage: motivational, slightly informal, works well in team preparation contexts.

• **Keep your eye on the ball:**

Meaning: to stay focused on the primary goal without being distracted by peripheral issues. Origin: sports, watching the ball at all times to maintain control.

Example: "There's going to be a lot of noise in this negotiation; keep your eye on the ball. Our priority is the contract length, not the rate."

Usage: a reminder to maintain strategic focus.

• **Lay your cards on the table:**

Meaning: to be fully transparent about your position, needs, or intentions.

Example: "I think the fastest path to a deal is to lay our cards on the table early; here's what we can offer and here's what we need."

Usage: signals honesty and good faith. Powerful because it's unexpected in **competitive negotiations.**

• **Know when to hold and when to fold:**

Meaning, to understand which concessions are acceptable and which cross a line, and to recognize when a deal is no longer worth pursuing.

Origin: poker.

Example: "Part of good negotiation is knowing when to hold and when to fold; not every deal is worth closing at any price."

Usage note: poker reference, explain briefly in international contexts if needed.

The Pre-Negotiation Strategy Checklist: Using Idioms as Framework

Before any significant negotiation, work through these questions using the idioms as your framework:

Have I covered all the bases?, List every topic the other party might raise. For each one, know your position, your ideal outcome, and your minimum acceptable outcome.

Do I have a plan B?, For each key issue, define what you'll do if your first proposal is rejected. Never enter a negotiation with only one option.

Am I ready to roll with the punches?, Identify the two or three scenarios you least expect. Decide in advance how you'll respond if they happen.

What's my A-game for this specific conversation?, What is the one argument, offer, or approach most likely to move this particular counterpart? That's where you lead.

What ball am I keeping my eye on?, Name your single most important outcome. When the conversation gets complicated, this is what you return to.

11.2 Closing the Deal: Idiomatic Expressions for Persuasion

Persuasion in negotiation is not manipulation, it is the art of helping the other party see the value in what you're proposing. The idioms below are used at the moments when the conversation shifts from exploration to commitment.

Persuasion Idioms

- **Seal the deal:**

Meaning: to finalize an agreement, to reach the point of commitment.

Example: "I think we're aligned on the key terms; what would it take to seal the deal today?"

Usage: signals readiness to conclude. Use when you genuinely sense the other party is close to yes.

- **Win-win:**

Meaning: an outcome where both parties gain something of value.

Example: "I want to make sure we structure this as a genuine win-win. I'm not interested in a deal that only works for one side."

Usage: signals collaborative intent. Extremely powerful early in a negotiation to set the tone.

- **Drive the point home:**

Meaning: to emphasize and reinforce your key argument until it is fully understood and remembered.

Example: "Let me drive this point home; every week of delay costs both of us, not just you."

Usage: use when your key argument risks being lost in discussion.

- **Cut to the chase:**

Meaning: to get directly to the essential point without preamble.

Example: "I appreciate the background, but let me cut to the chase; here's what we need to make this work."

Usage: signals confidence and respect for the other party's time.

- **See eye to eye:**

Meaning: to agree, to share the same view on something.

Example: "I think we see eye to eye on the quality standards; the question is whether we can align on the timeline."

Usage: builds rapport by identifying shared ground before addressing differences.

- **Sweeten the deal:**

Meaning: to add something extra to make an offer more attractive.

Example: "If we can sweeten the deal with an extended warranty period, I think that addresses your main concern."

Usage: signals flexibility and desire to reach agreement.

• Give and take:

Meaning: mutual concession, both parties offering and receiving something.

Example: "Any good negotiation involves give and take; here's what we're prepared to offer, and here's what we'd need in return."

Usage: frames concessions as normal and expected rather than as weakness.

• Show your hand:

Meaning: to reveal your true position, intentions, or limits.

Example: "I don't want to show my hand too early, but I can tell you we have significant flexibility on the payment terms."

Usage: strategic, often mentioned as something to avoid ("I don't want to show my hand") as much as something to do.

Negotiation Persuasion Arc: Idioms Through a Full Conversation

Opening: establish collaboration:

"Before we get into the details, I want to make sure we're approaching this as a win-win. We're genuinely committed to finding terms that work for both sides."

Building the argument:

"Let me drive this point home; the value we're bringing to this partnership is not just in the product but in the support and integration work that comes with it."

Moving toward agreement:

"I think we see eye to eye on the core terms. Can we talk about what it would take to sweeten the deal enough for you to move forward this week?"

Handling a hesitation:

"I understand the concern about the timeline. Let's cut to the chase — if we could guarantee delivery by the fifteenth, does that resolve the issue?"

Closing:

"I think we have everything we need here. What do you say — are we ready to seal the deal?"

11.3 Handling Objections: Idioms for Overcoming Resistance

Every negotiation will encounter resistance. An objection is not a rejection, it is information. The idioms below help you navigate that moment: staying calm, demonstrating flexibility, and keeping the conversation moving toward resolution.

Objection-Handling Idioms

• **Turn the tables:**

Meaning: to reverse the situation, to shift the advantage to your side.

Example: "When they raised the pricing objection, we turned the tables by showing the total cost of ownership versus the alternatives."

Usage: describes a strategic reframe, used more often to describe what happened than as something you say directly in the moment.

• **Play it by ear:**

Meaning: to respond flexibly based on how the situation develops, without a rigid script.

Example: "We don't know exactly how they'll respond to the revised terms; let's play it by ear and see where the conversation goes."

Usage: signals adaptability. Best in internal discussions rather than said directly to the other party.

• **Hear them out:**

Meaning: to listen fully to the other party's position or concern before responding.

Example: "Before we respond to the objection, let's hear them out completely; there may be something we're missing."

Usage: signals respect and active listening. Extremely effective for de-escalating resistance.

• **Clear the air:**

Meaning: to address misunderstandings or tension openly so they no longer block progress.

Example: "I'd like to take a moment to clear the air; I think there may be some confusion about what we're actually proposing here."

Usage: use when you sense the resistance is based on misunderstanding rather than genuine disagreement.

• **Stay the course:**

Meaning: to remain committed to your strategy despite pressure or setbacks.

Example: "They've pushed back three times on the exclusivity clause, but I think we should stay the course — it's a dealbreaker for us."

Usage: internal language, what you say to your team, not to the other party.

• **Stand your ground:**

Meaning: to maintain your position firmly despite pressure to concede.

Example: "On the payment terms, we need to stand our ground. We cannot extend to 90 days under any circumstances."

Usage: direct, signals clear limits.

• **Find a middle ground:**

Meaning: to reach a compromise position that partially satisfies both parties.

Example: "We can't go to sixty days, and you can't go to thirty. Let's find a middle ground at forty-five."

Usage: signals willingness to compromise without full capitulation.

• **Come to terms:**

Meaning: to reach a mutual agreement, to finalize the conditions of a deal.

Example: "After three rounds of discussion, we've finally come to terms on the pricing structure."

Usage: formal, signals concluded negotiation.

Handling a Difficult Objection: A Realistic Dialogue

Other party: "We've reviewed your proposal and frankly the pricing is significantly above what we budgeted."

Your response: "Thank you for being direct. Let's clear the air on that. The figure in the proposal includes full implementation support, which most competitors charge separately. Let me drive that point home: you're comparing our all-in price to their base price. That's not an apples-to-apples comparison."

Other party: "Even so, there's still a gap we need to address."

Your response: "I understand. I want to hear you out; what specifically is the gap, and is it purely about total cost or also about payment timing?"

Other party: "Primarily timing. If we could spread payments differently, the total would be more manageable."

Your response: "Now we're talking. There's definitely room for give and take on the payment structure. If we find a middle ground on timing that works for your cash flow, can we come to terms on the rest of the contract today?"

Chapter 11 Practice Exercises

Check your answers in the Answer Key at the back of the book.

Exercise 1: Negotiation Stage Identification

For each idiom below, identify which negotiation stage it fits best, Preparation (P), Persuasion (PE), or Objection Handling (O):

1. "Let's make sure we cover all the bases before the meeting." ___

2. "I think we can seal the deal if we adjust the timeline slightly." ___

3. "Before we respond, let's hear them out completely." ___

4. "We need a plan B in case they reject the initial offer." ___

5. "Let me drive this point home — the value is in the long-term partnership, not the upfront cost." ___

6. "On the exclusivity clause, we need to stand our ground." ___

7. "I want to approach this as a genuine win-win from the start." ___

8. "Let's clear the air about what the proposal actually includes." ___

Exercise 2: Choose the Right Idiom

Select the most appropriate idiom to complete each negotiation sentence:

1. "Before we go further, let me ___________________ — we cannot go below a twelve-month contract." (cut to the chase / roll with the punches / play it by ear)

2. "They've pushed back on the price, but I don't think we should concede yet — let's ___________________." (show our hand / stay the course / seal the deal)

3. "I think we're close. Is there anything we can do to ___________________ and get your sign-off today?" (sweeten the deal / turn the tables / cover all the bases)

4. "Before I respond to that concern, I want to make sure I understand it fully — can I
_______________________ first?" (stand my ground / hear you out / drive the point home)

5. "We can't meet their exact number and they can't meet ours — but I think we can
_______________________." (find a middle ground / roll with the punches / lay our cards
on the table)

Exercise 3: Negotiation Dialogue Completion

Complete the negotiation dialogue below by filling in the missing idiom from the box.
Each idiom should be used once.

Word Box: win-win / cut to the chase / see eye to eye / seal the deal / give and take /
cover all the bases

Negotiator A: "Before we begin, I want to say that our goal here is a genuine
_______________________. We're not looking to win at your expense."

Negotiator B: "We appreciate that. Let's _______________________ — what are the three
terms that matter most to you?"

Negotiator A: "Timeline, payment structure, and exclusivity. I think we
_______________________ on timeline. The other two need more discussion."

Negotiator B: "Agreed. Any good negotiation involves _______________________. We're
prepared to be flexible on payment if you'll consider adjusting the exclusivity window."

Negotiator A: "That's a reasonable basis for discussion. If we can
_______________________ all those issues today, I think we could _______________________
before the end of the week."

Exercise 4: Handling the Objection

Read the objection below. Write a professional response of 4–6 sentences that handles the
resistance using at least three idioms from section 11.3. Do not become defensive or make
immediate concessions, acknowledge, clarify, and redirect.

Objection: "We've used your service for two years and honestly we feel like we've been
taken for granted. The competitor is offering better terms and frankly we're considering
switching."

Your response:

____

____

____

Exercise 5: Cultural Adaptation in Negotiation

Three idioms in this chapter carry sports or game origins that may not translate clearly in international negotiations. For each one, write a plain-language alternative that carries the same meaning:

1. "Cover all the bases" (baseball origin):

Your alternative:

____

2. "Know when to hold and when to fold" (poker origin):

Your alternative:

____

3. "Roll with the punches" (boxing origin):

Your alternative:

____

Chapter Twelve

Idioms for Leadership and Management

Leadership is fundamentally an act of communication. Every decision a leader makes, every direction they set, every moment of accountability they hold, all of it is expressed through language. And the language of leadership in English-speaking professional environments is heavily idiomatic.

When a leader says "I need everyone to step up to the plate on this," they're communicating urgency, responsibility, and confidence in the team simultaneously, in eight words. When they say "let's see the big picture before we get lost in the details," they're setting a strategic frame for the entire conversation that follows.

For non-native English speakers in leadership roles, or aspiring to them, mastering this language is not optional. It is part of the job. This chapter covers three dimensions of leadership language: projecting authority and vision, motivating teams, and navigating change.

12.1 Leading with Confidence: Idioms for Effective Leadership

The most effective leadership idioms do something plain language struggles to do: they compress authority, direction, and cultural resonance into a single expression. A leader who says "I'm going to take the bull by the horns on this" signals courage, decisiveness, and personal ownership in six words. That same message in plain language takes a sentence, and loses the energy.

Core Leadership Authority Idioms

• **Call the shots:**

Meaning: to be the decision-maker, to have the authority to determine what happens.

Example: "In this project, the product team calls the shots on the feature set; engineering takes the lead on implementation."

Usage: establishes clear authority and decision ownership. Important in matrix organizations where responsibility can be ambiguous.

• **Take the bull by the horns:**

Meaning: to confront a challenge directly and with courage rather than avoiding or delaying. Example: "We've been dancing around the performance issue for three months; it's time to take the bull by the horns and have the conversation."

Usage: signals decisive leadership action. Appropriate when the team needs to see courage modeled.

• **See the big picture:**

Meaning: to understand the broader context and long-term implications beyond the immediate situation.

Example: "I know the short-term numbers are concerning, but let's see the big picture — this investment will pay off by Q3 next year."

Usage: essential for strategic communication. Distinguishes leadership from management.

• **Stay the course:**

Meaning: to maintain direction and commitment despite pressure, setbacks, or temptation to change.

Example: "I know there's pressure from the board to pivot, but I believe we should stay the course — our strategy is sound and the market is moving our way."

Usage: requires confidence and clear rationale, without both, "stay the course" sounds like stubbornness.

• **Lead by example:**

Meaning: to demonstrate through your own behavior the standards and conduct you expect from others.

Example: "If we want a culture of accountability, leadership has to lead by example; that starts with how we handle our own missed deadlines."

Usage: one of the most powerful leadership idioms, and the most demanding, because it is a personal commitment.

- **Walk the talk:**

Meaning: to ensure your actions are consistent with your words and stated values.

Example: "We say we value work-life balance, but our senior leaders are sending emails at midnight — we need to walk the talk."

Usage: often used to call out gaps between stated values and observed behavior. Use carefully, it can feel confrontational.

- **Set the tone:**

Meaning: to establish the atmosphere, standards, or culture through early behavior and decisions.

Example: "The first week of a new project sets the tone for everything that follows; I want us to be rigorous, communicative, and on time from day one."

Usage: leadership communication at transitions, new projects, new teams, new years.

- **Keep a level head:**

Meaning: to remain calm, rational, and composed under pressure.

Example: "When the system went down on launch day, it was critical that the team leads kept a level head; panic spreads faster than solutions." Usage: describes composure under pressure. Important for leaders in crisis situations.

Leadership Language in Context: Three Scenarios

Scenario 1: Starting a new project:

"I want to set the tone right from the start. We're going to lead by example on every commitment we make — if we say something will be done by Friday, it will be done by Friday. We need to see the big picture even when we're deep in the details, and when things get hard — and they will — we stay the course."

Scenario 2: Addressing a team performance issue:

"I've been observing the situation for a while, and it's time to take the bull by the horns. There are some accountability gaps on this team that we haven't addressed directly. Going forward, I'll be calling the shots on how we track deliverables — and I'll be doing it alongside you, not above you. I need to walk the talk on this too."

Scenario 3: Under pressure from above:

"I know there's pressure to change our approach. But I want us to keep a level head here and see the big picture. The data supports what we're doing. My recommendation to the team is that we stay the course and let the results speak."

12.2 Motivating Your Team: Idioms for Inspiring Action

Motivation is not a single conversation: it's an ongoing practice embedded in the daily language of leadership. The idioms below are the expressions leaders use to ignite energy, acknowledge effort, and sustain momentum through the difficult middle of any project.

Motivational Leadership Idioms

• Go the extra mile:

Meaning: to do more than is required or expected, to invest additional effort in the pursuit of excellence.

Example: "What separates this team from the competition is that we consistently go the extra mile for our clients; and they notice."

Usage: one of the most universally understood motivational expressions, works in virtually every professional culture.

• Rise to the occasion:

Meaning: to perform exceptionally well when the stakes are high or the challenge is significant.

Example: "I've seen this team rise to the occasion before; I have no doubt you'll do it again on this launch."

Usage: most powerful at moments of challenge or uncertainty, a leader's expression of confidence in the team.

• Step up to the plate:

Meaning: to take responsibility, to volunteer for a challenge, to perform when performance is needed. Origin: baseball, the batter stepping up when it's their turn.

Example: "I need someone to step up to the plate and lead the client relationship while Priya is on leave."

Usage note: baseball origin, may need brief explanation in non-American contexts.

• Keep the momentum going:

Meaning: to maintain the energy, progress, and forward movement already established.

Example: "We've had an incredible first quarter; the challenge now is to keep the momentum going through the summer months."

Usage: most effective immediately after a success, to prevent complacency.

• **Light a fire under:**

Meaning: to motivate someone urgently, to push someone into faster action.

Example: "The team needs someone to light a fire under the development timeline; we're two weeks behind and the client is watching."

Usage: informal, use carefully. Can feel aggressive if the relationship is not established.

• **Pull out all the stops:**

Meaning: to use every available resource and effort, to hold nothing back.

Origin: pipe organ, pulling out all the stops produces maximum volume.

Example: "For this pitch, I want us to pull out all the stops; this is the client that changes everything if we win it."

Usage: signals the highest level of commitment and resource allocation.

• **Sink or swim:**

Meaning: to face a challenge without assistance, where success or failure depends entirely on one's own efforts.

Example: "The new hires are being given real projects from week one; it's a sink or swim environment, but it produces our best people."

Usage: describes a high-expectations culture. Use carefully, can seem unsupportive if not accompanied by clear framework.

• **Run a tight ship:**

Meaning: to manage a team or organization with discipline, efficiency, and high standards.

Example: "Our operations manager runs a tight ship; every process is documented, every deadline is tracked, every standard is maintained."

Usage: strong praise for management quality and operational discipline.

Motivational Language Through a Difficult Project

Week 1: Project launch:

"I want everyone to hit the ground running on this. We have eight weeks, and every one of them matters. This team has risen to the occasion before — I'm expecting the same here."

Week 4: Mid-project difficulty:

"I know it's been a grinding few weeks. But we need to keep the momentum going — we're past the hardest part. This is exactly the moment where this team has always gone the extra mile."

Week 7: Final push:

"One week left. I need everyone to pull out all the stops. The client is watching, the business is watching, and honestly, I want this win for all of you — you've earned it."

12.3 Navigating Change: Idioms for Managing Transitions

Change is where leadership is most visibly tested. How a leader communicates during transitions, restructures, strategic pivots, leadership changes, market disruptions, determines whether their team moves through change with confidence or anxiety. The right idiomatic language provides clarity, signals stability, and frames change as opportunity rather than threat.

Change Management Idioms

• **Turn the page:**

Meaning: to move past something and begin a new chapter, leaving previous difficulties or failures behind.

Example: "The product launch didn't go as planned, but the market has spoken and it's time to turn the page and focus on what's next."

Usage: forward-looking and generous, implies the past is acknowledged and released.

• **Steer the ship:**

Meaning: to guide the organization through a period of uncertainty or change with control and direction.

Example: "In the absence of the CEO, the COO will be steering the ship; all strategic decisions go through her office."

Usage: implies steady, experienced leadership at the helm.

• **Have a game plan:**

Meaning: to have a clear, thought-through strategy ready before beginning.

Example: "Before we announce the restructuring, I want to make sure we have a game plan for every question employees might ask."

Usage: signals preparation and professional readiness.

• Shake things up:

Meaning: to make significant changes to existing processes, structures, or ways of working, often intentionally disruptive.

Example: "The new director has made clear she wants to shake things up in the operations division; expect some significant changes in Q2."

Usage: can signal positive disruption or negative instability depending on tone and context.

• Chart a new course:

Meaning: to set a fundamentally new direction or strategy.

Example: "After fifteen years in retail, the board has decided it's time to chart a new course and shift focus to digital-first channels."

Usage: formal and strategic, appropriate for major announcements and transitions.

• Bend but don't break:

Meaning: to remain resilient under pressure, adapting without abandoning core values or fundamental integrity.

Example: "Our philosophy through this restructuring is bend but don't break; we'll adapt our structure, but we will not compromise on quality or culture."

Usage: signals principled flexibility, powerful in change communications.

• Weather the storm:

Meaning: to endure and survive a period of difficulty, uncertainty, or crisis.

Example: "We've weathered storms before — the 2008 financial crisis, the supply chain disruptions of 2021; and we came out stronger each time."

Usage: builds confidence through historical resilience. Most powerful when paired with specific examples.

• The dust will settle:

Meaning: that after a period of uncertainty and disruption, clarity and stability will return.

Example: "I know there's a lot of uncertainty right now. The dust will settle; and when it does, I believe we'll find ourselves in a stronger position."

Usage: reassuring, forward-looking. Essential in periods of significant change.

Change Communication: A Model Leadership Message

"Team, I want to talk directly about what's happening and what it means for us.

The market has changed faster than any of us anticipated. It's time to turn the page on the strategy we launched eighteen months ago and chart a new course, one that reflects the reality we're operating in today.

I know change of this scale feels unsettling. But I want you to know that we've weathered storms before, and we'll weather this one too. Our job now is to steer the ship steadily through the transition, and I have a game plan for how we do that.

Here's what I need from you: bend but don't break. Adapt to what's changing, but hold onto what makes this team exceptional. The dust will settle, and when it does, we will be stronger and better positioned than we are today.

This is the moment to lead by example and go the extra mile. I'll be doing the same."

Notice how eight idioms appear in a short leadership message, each one earning its place by compressing a complex sentiment into a memorable expression.

Chapter 12 Practice Exercises

Check your answers in the Answer Key at the back of the book.

Exercise 1: Leadership Context Match

For each idiom below, identify which leadership context it fits best, Authority and Vision (AV), Motivation (M), or Change Management (CM):

1. "It's time to chart a new course for the division." ____

2. "I need someone to step up to the plate on the client relationship." ____

3. "Leadership has to walk the talk on work-life balance." ____

4. "We've weathered storms before — we'll get through this one." ____

5. "The team needs to pull out all the stops for this pitch." ____

6. "My job is to steer the ship while the restructuring unfolds." ____

7. "Let's see the big picture before we make this decision." ____

8. "Keep the momentum going — we're past the hardest part." ____

Exercise 2: Choose the Right Idiom

Select the most appropriate idiom for each leadership situation:

1. You want to acknowledge a team member who consistently does more than expected.

Best idiom: (go the extra mile / call the shots / shake things up)

2. You are announcing a significant new strategic direction to your organization.

Best idiom: (steer the ship / chart a new course / keep the momentum going)

3. You want to signal that your team should expect demanding standards and tight processes from you.

Best idiom: (light a fire under / run a tight ship / turn the page)

4. You want to reassure a nervous team that stability will return after a difficult period.

Best idiom: (the dust will settle / lead by example / rise to the occasion)

5. You want to inspire the team to perform at their highest level for a critical client pitch.

Best idiom: (stay the course / walk the talk / pull out all the stops)

Exercise 3: Write a Leadership Address

You are a team leader addressing your team at the start of a challenging quarter. Sales are down, two team members have left, and the team morale is low, but the fundamentals of the business remain strong.

Write a 8–10 sentence motivational address using at least six idioms from this chapter. Your address should:

- Acknowledge the difficulty honestly without catastrophizing
- Express confidence in the team's ability to rise to the challenge
- Set a clear direction and tone for the quarter ahead
- Close with a forward-looking and energizing statement

Your address:

____

____

____

Exercise 4: Leadership Idiom Formality Check

Some leadership idioms are appropriate for formal communications such as board presentations and company-wide announcements. Others work better in informal team settings. Rate each idiom below as Formal (F), Neutral (N), or Informal (I):

1. "Chart a new course" ____

2. "Light a fire under" ____

3. "Lead by example" ____

4. "Sink or swim" ____

5. "Steer the ship" ____

6. "Step up to the plate" ____

7. "Bend but don't break" ____

8. "Walk the talk" ____

Exercise 5: Cultural Adaptation

Three idioms in this chapter have sports or physical activity origins that may need explanation in international contexts. Write a plain-language alternative for each:

1. "Step up to the plate" (baseball origin):

Your alternative:

____

2. "Pull out all the stops" (pipe organ origin, less widely known):

Your alternative:

____

3. "Sink or swim" (may feel harsh in cultures that value collaborative support):

Your alternative:

____

Idioms for Cross-Cultural Communication

You are in a meeting with colleagues from Japan, Brazil, Germany, and Nigeria. The conversation is in English, but the English in that room sounds different depending on who is speaking, what they expect from communication, and how they interpret what they hear.

When an American colleague says "let's cut to the chase," a German colleague may feel relieved, that's their communication preference. A Japanese colleague may feel slightly uncomfortable, it signals a lack of respect for process. A Brazilian colleague may see it as abrupt and wonder if something is wrong. The same three words, three completely different experiences.

This is the core challenge of cross-cultural communication: language is not just language. It is culture encoded in words. Idioms carry this cultural encoding more densely than almost any other form of expression, which makes them both powerful and risky in international settings.

This chapter gives you the tools to use idioms across cultural contexts skillfully: which expressions are genuinely universal, which need care, which to avoid entirely in international settings, and how to build the cultural intelligence that underpins all of it.

13.1 Universal Idioms: Expressions That Travel Well

Not all idioms are equally risky in cross-cultural settings. Some expressions have become so widely adopted through global business culture, English language education, and international media that they are genuinely understood across most professional contexts worldwide.

These are your safest tools in international communication.

High-Safety Idioms for International Settings

• On the same page:

Meaning: sharing the same understanding. Risk level: very low. This expression appears in English language education globally and is understood across cultures.

Example: "Before we proceed, I want to make sure we're all on the same page on the objectives."

• The bottom line:

Meaning: the most important point or the final financial result. Risk level: very low. Widely used across cultures in both literal financial contexts and figurative ones.

Example: "The bottom line is that we need to make a decision by Friday."

• Find common ground:

Meaning: to identify shared interests or areas of agreement. Risk level: very low. The concept of finding shared ground is universal across cultures and business contexts.

Example: "I believe we can find common ground on the pricing if we look at it from a different angle."

• Move forward:

Meaning: to proceed, to take the next step. Risk level: very low. Simple, literal enough to be clear, and widely understood.

Example: "Are we ready to move forward on the proposal?"

• Follow up:

Meaning: to check on the progress of something or make contact again. Risk level: very low. Standard in global business English education.

Example: "I'll follow up with you next week to see where things stand."

• In the loop:

Meaning: informed and included in relevant communications. Risk level: low. Widely used and generally understood.

Example: "Please keep me in the loop as the project develops."

• **The big picture:**

Meaning: the overall situation or long-term view. Risk level: low. Used broadly in English language education worldwide.

Example: "Let's step back and look at the big picture before we make this decision."

• **Win-win:**

Meaning: an outcome beneficial to all parties. Risk level: very low. This expression appears in negotiation training worldwide.

Example: "I think we can structure this as a genuine win-win for both organizations."

• **Touch base:**

Meaning: to make brief contact to check in or update. Risk level: moderate. Widely understood but more natural in American/British English contexts, some non-native speakers may not know it.

Example: "Let's touch base after you've had time to review the proposal."

• **Go the extra mile:**

Meaning: to do more than expected. Risk level: low. The concept and the expression are well understood across many cultures.

Example: "This team consistently goes the extra mile for our clients."

Why These Travel Well

These expressions share common characteristics: they are taught in standard business English curricula worldwide, they appear frequently in global media and publications, their imagery is either literal enough to understand or abstract enough not to cause confusion, and they encode universal concepts, alignment, outcomes, relationships, rather than culturally specific references.

13.2 Respecting Cultural Nuances: Idioms for Global Etiquette

Beyond choosing the right idioms, effective cross-cultural communication requires understanding how different cultures experience the same conversation, and adjusting your approach accordingly.

High-Risk Idiom Categories in International Settings

Sports idioms: American sports references:

Expressions like "home run," "touchdown," "slam dunk," "knock it out of the park," "Monday morning quarterback," and "cover all the bases" draw on American sports that are not widely followed outside North America. In meetings with international colleagues, these can cause genuine confusion or make the speaker seem culturally unaware.

Safe alternative strategy: replace with plain language. "That was an outstanding result" replaces "home run." "Let's make sure we've prepared for every scenario" replaces "cover all the bases."

Military and violence idioms:

Expressions like "bite the bullet," "call in the cavalry," "under fire," and "jump ship" draw on military imagery that can feel aggressive or inappropriate in cultures where military references carry political weight or historical sensitivity.

Safe alternative strategy: use when the meaning is well-established and the audience is international business professionals, but be ready to paraphrase if you see any uncertainty.

Idioms with different meanings across English variants:

As discussed in Chapter 5, "table the discussion" means opposite things in American and British English. "Quite good" in British English means something significantly different from American usage. These are invisible traps for speakers who assume all English is the same.

Safe alternative strategy: when working with mixed English-variant teams, default to the plainest possible version of your meaning.

Idioms implying negative judgment:

Expressions like "barking up the wrong tree," "spill the beans," or "let the cat out of the bag" can feel accusatory or informal in cultures where indirect communication is the norm. In high-context cultures, Japan, South Korea, many Middle Eastern and Southeast Asian contexts, these idioms can feel blunt to the point of rudeness.

Safe alternative strategy: in formal international contexts, deliver feedback and observations in plain language rather than idiom.

Cultural Communication Styles and Idiom Use

Different cultures have fundamentally different communication norms, and understanding these helps you choose not just which idioms to use, but how much idiomatic language to use at all.

Low-context cultures: Germany, Netherlands, Scandinavia, USA:

Communication is direct, explicit, and expects words to carry the full meaning. Idioms are generally acceptable, especially those that add efficiency. These audiences appreciate "cut to the chase" and "the bottom line."

High-context cultures: Japan, South Korea, China, many Arab cultures:

Communication relies heavily on implicit understanding, relationship context, and what is left unsaid. Too many idioms can feel alienating or exclusionary. In these settings, fewer idioms and simpler language shows respect. When idioms are used, they should be those that are widely taught in English education.

Relationship-first cultures: Brazil, Mexico, much of Latin America and the Middle East:

Business is built on personal relationships before professional transactions. Idioms that signal warmth and human connection, "we're in the same boat," "let's find common ground," "break the ice", are valued. Idioms that signal impatience or transactional focus, "cut to the chase," "get to the point", can feel rude before a relationship is established.

Formal cultures: UK, Japan, Germany, many European contexts:

Highly informal idioms: "ping me," "hop on a call," "shoot me an email", can feel disrespectful in formal professional relationships. Read the formality level of the relationship before deploying informal idioms.

Etiquette Idioms: Navigating Global Courtesy

• **Mind your P's and Q's:**

Meaning: to pay careful attention to politeness, manners, and appropriate behavior.

Example: "In any new cultural context, it pays to mind your P's and Q's until you understand the norms."

Usage note: widely understood in British and American English, may need explaining in other contexts.

• **When in Rome, do as the Romans do:**

Meaning, adapt to the customs and practices of the place or culture you are in.

Example: "Before the Tokyo meetings, I'd recommend spending time understanding business card etiquette — when in Rome."

Usage: signals cultural respect and adaptability.

- **Walk a mile in someone else's shoes:**

Meaning, to try to understand another person's perspective and experience before judging.

Example: "Before we assess how the rollout affected the regional teams, let's try to walk a mile in their shoes."

Usage: universally positive, signals empathy and respect.

- **Read between the lines:**

Meaning: to understand the implied or unstated meaning beyond the literal words.

Example: "In the meeting, the client said everything was 'fine'; but you need to read between the lines. They had concerns."

Usage: essential in high-context cultures where what is not said is as important as what is.

- **Tread lightly:**

Meaning: to approach a sensitive topic or situation with great care and caution.

Example: "This is a politically sensitive topic within their organization; we should tread lightly in how we raise it."

Usage: appropriate when navigating sensitive topics across cultural boundaries.

13.3 Building Cultural Competence: Idioms for Inclusivity

Cultural competence in language means more than avoiding offensive idioms. It means actively choosing language that includes, rather than excludes, that signals to every person in the room that they belong in this conversation.

Inclusivity

Idioms

- **We're all in the same boat:**

Meaning: everyone faces the same challenges and is working toward the same outcome.

Example: "I know the new reporting requirements feel like extra work; we're all in the same boat on this one." Inclusivity value: removes hierarchy from shared difficulty. Everyone is equal in the challenge.

- **Many hands make light work:**

Meaning: tasks are easier and more manageable when everyone contributes.

Example: "The data migration is a big task, but with the full team involved; many hands make light work." Inclusivity value: signals that every contribution, regardless of role or seniority, matters.

- **Two heads are better than one: Meaning:**

collaboration and diverse perspectives produce better outcomes than any single person's thinking.

Example: "I'd like to hear your perspective on this before I finalize my recommendation; two heads are better than one."

Inclusivity value: explicitly invites collaboration and validates the other person's contribution.

- **A rising tide lifts all boats:**

Meaning: when one person or group succeeds, it creates conditions for collective improvement.

Example: "Our goal is not to win market share from each other; a rising tide lifts all boats, and growing the overall market benefits everyone."

Inclusivity value: reframes individual success as collective benefit.

- **Variety is the spice of life:**

Meaning: diversity and difference make experiences richer and more valuable.

Example: "I love that this team brings together so many different professional backgrounds; variety is the spice of life, and it shows in the quality of our thinking."

Inclusivity value: celebrates rather than tolerates diversity.

- **Keep an open mind:**

Meaning: to be genuinely receptive to new ideas, approaches, or perspectives without judgment.

Example: "I'm going to ask you to keep an open mind during this presentation; some of what I'm proposing is unconventional."

Inclusivity value: creates psychological safety for difference and innovation.

- **Bring to the table:**

Meaning: to contribute something of value to a discussion or collaboration.

Example: "I want to make sure every member of this team knows what unique expertise they bring to the table."

Inclusivity value: positions everyone as a contributor, not just the loudest voices.

A Framework for Cross-Cultural Idiom Use

Before using any idiom in an international professional context, run through this quick assessment:

1. Is my audience familiar with this expression?, If uncertain, default to plain language.

2. Does this idiom contain a cultural reference specific to one country?, Sports, military, food, historical events. If yes, find a plain alternative.

3. What is the communication style of this culture?, High-context or low-context, direct or indirect, formal or informal.

4. Does this idiom signal inclusion or exclusion?, Does it bring people together or create an in-group that not everyone is part of?

5. If I had to explain this idiom, would the explanation embarrass me?, If yes, it probably doesn't belong in this context.

Chapter 13 Practice Exercises

Check your answers in the Answer Key at the back of the book.

Exercise 1: Safe or Risky?

Rate each idiom below for use in a formal international meeting with participants from Japan, Germany, Brazil, and the United Arab Emirates. Rate as Safe (S), Use with Care (C), or Avoid (A):

1. "We're all on the same page." ____

2. "Let's cover all the bases before the meeting." ____

3. "The bottom line is we need a decision by Friday." ____

4. "That was a real home run for the team." ____

5. "Let's find common ground on the pricing." ____

6. "We should table this discussion." ___

7. "I'd love to pick your brain about the regional market." ___

8. "A rising tide lifts all boats." ___

Exercise 2: Cultural Communication Style Match

Match each communication style characteristic with the correct cultural category:

Characteristics:

1. Prefers direct, explicit communication where words carry the full meaning ___

2. Values relationship-building before business, warmth and connection matter ___

3. Communication relies on implied meaning and what is left unsaid ___

4. Formal professional relationships: informal idioms feel disrespectful ___

Categories:

A. High-context cultures (Japan, South Korea, China)

B. Low-context cultures (Germany, Netherlands, USA)

C. Relationship-first cultures (Brazil, Mexico, much of Latin America)

D. Formal cultures (UK, Germany, many European contexts)

Exercise 3: Replace the Risky Idiom

Each sentence below contains an idiom that could cause confusion or offense in an international context. Rewrite each sentence replacing the idiom with plain language that preserves the meaning:

1. "We need to cover all the bases before the client presentation."

Your rewrite:

____

2. "That campaign was a real slam dunk for the marketing team."

Your rewrite:

____

3. "Let's table the budget discussion until next week."

Your rewrite:

____

4. "I think we need to bite the bullet on the pricing decision."

Your rewrite:

Exercise 4: Inclusivity Idiom Application

Choose the most appropriate inclusivity idiom from section 13.3 to complete each sentence:

1. "I know the workload seems overwhelming, but _______________ — if everyone contributes, we'll get through it much faster." (many hands make light work / tread lightly / a rising tide lifts all boats)

2. "I'm proposing a new approach — I just ask that you _______________." (walk a mile in their shoes / keep an open mind / read between the lines)

3. "Every person on this team has something unique to _______________ — I want to make sure we're hearing from everyone." (bring to the table / find common ground / go the extra mile)

4. "This isn't a zero-sum competition between our divisions — _______________ here." (when in Rome / a rising tide lifts all boats / two heads are better than one)

Exercise 5: Cross-Cultural Communication Plan

You are preparing for a series of meetings with a new business partner based in Tokyo. The relationship is new and formal. You know that Japanese business culture is high-context, values process and respect, and tends toward indirect communication.

Write a short paragraph (5–7 sentences) describing how you would adjust your use of idiomatic language for these meetings. Address:

• Which types of idioms you would use and which you would avoid

• How you would handle situations where you need to deliver difficult feedback

• What cultural awareness principles would guide your communication

Your paragraph:

____

____

____

Chapter Fourteen

Avoiding Common Pitfalls

I dioms don't fail because learners don't know them. They fail because learners use the right expression in the wrong context, the wrong formality level, the wrong audience, the wrong cultural setting, or at the wrong moment in a conversation.

This chapter is your error-prevention toolkit. It covers the most common ways idiomatic language goes wrong, and the specific strategies that prevent each type of failure. By the end, you'll have a clear decision framework for evaluating any idiom before you use it, and a practical understanding of the most common mistakes to avoid.

14.1 Formality Failures: Using the Wrong Idiom in the Wrong Setting

The most common idiom mistake in professional settings is not using an expression incorrectly, it's using a casual expression in a formal context, or being unnecessarily formal when informal language would build better rapport.

The Formality Spectrum

Understanding where an expression sits on the formality spectrum is the first step to using it correctly. Here is the full range, with examples at each level:

Highly Formal: legal documents, regulatory submissions, board reports, executive communications:

Appropriate idioms: "in light of," "with reference to," "for your consideration," "we are committed to," "at your earliest convenience"

Inappropriate idioms: anything conversational, "touch base," "circle back," "get the ball rolling," "shoot me an email"

Formal: client proposals, senior external emails, first professional contact:

Appropriate idioms: "the bottom line," "move forward," "put our best foot forward," "leave no stone unturned," "seal the deal"

Inappropriate idioms: highly casual expressions, "ping me," "hop on a call," "shoot the breeze," "off the cuff"

Neutral: standard professional emails, internal reports, regular team meetings:

Appropriate idioms: "touch base," "circle back," "on the same page," "follow up," "get the ball rolling," "in the loop"

Inappropriate idioms: highly informal expressions, "shoot me a message," "what's the deal," "no-brainer"

Informal: trusted colleague messages, casual team communication, instant messaging:

Appropriate idioms: "ping me," "hop on a call," "circle back," "let's jam on this," "shoot me an email"

Inappropriate idioms: highly formal language that creates unnecessary distance

Idioms That Commonly Land in the Wrong Register

The following idioms are frequently misplaced, used in formal contexts where they feel out of place, or in formal communications where they undermine credibility:

• "Shoot the breeze":

Means to chat casually about nothing important. Almost never appropriate in professional written communication. A board meeting is not the place for this idiom.

• **"Off the cuff":**

Means without preparation. Using this in a formal presentation context signals a lack of preparation, the opposite of what you want.

Example of wrong use: "Off the cuff, I'd say our revenue projection is around twelve million."

Better: "Based on our current trajectory, the revenue projection is approximately twelve million."

- **"Cut corners":**

Means to do something in the cheapest or easiest way possible, often at the expense of quality. Using this in a proposal, even to say you won't cut corners, introduces a negative association.

Better to avoid it in written formal documents entirely.

- **"Bite the dust":**

Means to fail or die. Jarring in professional contexts, especially when discussing a project that has not succeeded.

Better alternatives: "the initiative did not achieve its objectives," "we've discontinued the project."

- "Throw in the towel":

Means to give up entirely. Used casually, this is fine. In a formal status report, it signals surrender rather than strategic reorientation.

Better: "we've made the decision to pivot the strategy based on new market data."

- "Shoot from the hip":

Means to act or speak without thinking. Almost always implies a lack of preparation. Avoid in formal settings.

Better: "I'll give you my initial thinking and follow up with a more considered assessment."

The Four Questions Before You Use an Idiom

Before using any idiom in professional communication, ask:

1. Who is my audience?, Native speaker or non-native? Senior or peer? Familiar or first contact?

2. What is the context?, Formal document, professional email, team meeting, casual conversation?

3. What is the cultural background?, American, British, international mixed, high-context, low-context?

4. What is the emotional tone?, Tense and serious, collaborative and warm, urgent and action-focused?

If the idiom fits all four: use it with confidence. If it fits two or three, adapt or explain. If it fits one or none, use plain language instead.

14.2 Understanding Idiom Variations: When and Where to Use Them

Beyond formality, idioms can backfire because the same expression means different things in different English-speaking regions, or because an expression that is well established in one era sounds outdated in another.

Regional Variation Pitfalls

As established in Chapter 5, "table the discussion" is the most dangerous regional variation, meaning opposite things in American and British English. But it is not alone.

Additional regional pitfalls:

• **"Knock on wood" (American) vs. "Touch wood" (British):**
Same superstitious meaning, but using the wrong version in the wrong country sounds odd. In international contexts, neither is necessary, plain language works better.

• **"Push the envelope" (American) vs. "Push the boat out" (British):** Both suggest going beyond conventional limits, but "push the boat out" in Britain also means to celebrate extravagantly, which can cause confusion in strategic discussions.

• **"Quite good", a significant transatlantic trap:**
In American English, "quite good" means very good. In British English, "quite good" is damning with faint praise, it means passable but not impressive. This is not an idiom per se, but it follows the same principle: English words carry different cultural weights depending on the speaker.

• **"I could care less" vs. "I couldn't care less":**
This is one of the most common idiomatic errors even among native speakers. "I couldn't care less" is correct, meaning I have zero care left to give. "I could care less" (the common American version) is technically the opposite, though widely understood. In formal professional writing, always use "couldn't."

Outdated Idioms: When an Expression Has Aged Out

Some idioms were once standard but now read as dated, clichéd, or out of touch. Using them in professional communications can undermine your credibility with native speakers who recognize them as overused:

Overused to the point of cliché: use sparingly or avoid:

• "Think outside the box": Once innovative, now the first example given when discussing business clichés. If you must convey this idea, say "approach this differently" or "challenge the conventional assumptions."

• "Low-hanging fruit": Widely understood but overused. Consider "the easiest wins" or "the most accessible opportunities."

• "Move the needle": Still acceptable but becoming tired. Consider "make a meaningful difference" or "produce measurable results."

• "At the end of the day": Filler phrase that adds nothing. Remove it from your writing entirely.

• "Going forward": Often unnecessary. "From now on" or simply removing the phrase works equally well.

• "Touch base": Still useful, but so overused in corporate settings that some people react negatively. In writing, "connect briefly" or "follow up" is often cleaner.

14.3 Common Missteps: Idioms That Can Backfire

Some idioms fail not because of register or region, but because their imagery is too vivid, too negative, or too easily misunderstood in professional contexts.

High-Risk Idioms in Professional Settings

• **"Kick the bucket":** Means to die. Never appropriate in professional communication, even humorously. There is no business context where this expression adds value.

• **"Get the wrong end of the stick":** Means to misunderstand completely. The expression itself can cause confusion because of its unusual imagery. Better: "I think there may have been a misunderstanding" or "let me clarify what I meant."

• **"Bite the bullet"**: Useful in many contexts, but the military/pain imagery can land poorly in formal written communications or with audiences unfamiliar with the origin. In those cases, "accept the difficult decision" or "commit to the harder path" works better.

• **"Stab in the back"**: Means to betray. The violent imagery is jarring in professional contexts. Better: "a breach of trust" or "a significant betrayal of the agreed terms."

• **"Lose your shirt"**: Means to lose all your money. Too casual for formal financial discussions. Better: "incur significant financial losses" or "face substantial financial exposure."

• **"Not my circus, not my monkeys"**: Means this is not my responsibility or problem. While increasingly common, this expression can sound dismissive and unprofessional, especially if the listener isn't familiar with the idiom's origin. Better: "this falls outside my remit" or "that's best handled by the relevant team."

How to Recover When an Idiom Misses

Even with the best preparation, you will occasionally use an idiom that doesn't land. Here is how to handle it without making it worse:

If you see confusion in the listener's face or response:

Immediately paraphrase in plain language: don't wait for them to ask. "What I mean by that is..." followed by a clear plain-language version resolves 95% of idiom misunderstandings instantly.

If you used the wrong register and the meeting feels more formal than expected:

Adjust your language for the rest of the conversation. You don't need to address it, just recalibrate and move forward with more formal language.

If you used an idiom that accidentally caused offense:

Acknowledge it directly and briefly: "I want to make sure that expression didn't come across the wrong way — what I meant was..." Then continue. Dwelling on it creates more discomfort than the original error.

If the idiom was simply wrong or misused:

Correct yourself naturally: "Actually, let me rephrase that..." followed by the correct expression or a plain-language version.

The cardinal rule: one immediate, clear correction is always better than hoping no one noticed, because someone always does.

Chapter 14 Practice Exercises

Check your answers in the Answer Key at the back of the book.

Exercise 1: Formality Spectrum Placement

Place each idiom in the correct formality category, Highly Formal (HF), Formal (F), Neutral (N), or Informal (I):

1. "With reference to your letter of March 12th..." ___

2. "Let's touch base after the weekend." ___

3. "Ping me when the report is ready." ___

4. "The bottom line is we need a decision today." ___

5. "We are committed to delivering the highest standard of service." ___

6. "Let's hop on a call this afternoon." ___

7. "In light of the recent market changes, we have revised our approach." ___

8. "Get the ball rolling on the onboarding paperwork." ___

Exercise 2: Wrong Register Identification

Each sentence below contains an idiom used in the wrong context. Identify the problem and rewrite the sentence with a more appropriate expression:

1. In a board presentation: "Off the cuff, I'd say we're looking at a fifteen percent growth target for next year."

Problem:

____

Rewrite:

____

2. In a formal client proposal: "We won't cut corners on this engagement — quality is everything."

Problem:

____

Rewrite:

____

3. In a performance review with a junior team member: "I'm concerned that you've been shooting from the hip on client communications."

Problem:

____

Rewrite:

____

Exercise 3: Cliché Alert

The following idioms have become so overused that they often undermine rather than enhance professional communication. Rewrite each sentence by replacing the cliché with fresh, plain language that conveys the same meaning:

1. "At the end of the day, what matters most is client satisfaction."

Your rewrite:

____

2. "We should focus on the low-hanging fruit before tackling the bigger challenges."

Your rewrite:

____

3. "Think outside the box; we need some genuinely new ideas here."

Your rewrite:

____

4. "Going forward, all expense reports must be submitted within 48 hours."

Your rewrite:

____

Exercise 4: Recovery Scripts

For each situation below, write a natural, professional recovery response:

1. You used the expression "throw in the towel" in a formal status meeting and your manager's expression showed concern.

Your recovery:

____

2. You used "bite the bullet" in an email to a new international client and they responded asking what you meant.

Your recovery:

____

3. You said "not my circus, not my monkeys" casually to a colleague and immediately regretted it when you saw their reaction.

Your recovery:

____

Exercise 5: The Four-Question Framework

Apply the four-question framework from section 14.1 to decide whether each idiom is appropriate for the scenario described. Write Use (U), Adapt (A), or Avoid (AV) for each:

Scenario: You are writing a formal proposal to a new client in Tokyo. The client is Japanese, English is not their first language, and this is your first professional contact.

1. "We want to put our best foot forward on this engagement." ___

2. "The bottom line is that we can deliver within your timeline." ___

3. "Let's touch base early next week to discuss the details." ___

4. "We'll go the extra mile to ensure your satisfaction." ___

5. "We'll cut to the chase — here are the three key deliverables." ___

Chapter Fifteen

Sustaining Your Learning Journey

Y ou've reached the final chapter. Take a moment to appreciate that, because getting here means you've done something most language learners never do: you've worked through a complete, systematic approach to one of the hardest aspects of English fluency.

But here's the truth about idiomatic language: it doesn't end with a book. Native speakers continue learning new expressions, adapting to new registers, and encountering idioms they've never heard before, throughout their entire professional lives. Language is alive. It grows, shifts, absorbs new influences, and occasionally retires old expressions.

What you're building isn't a fixed vocabulary list. It's a practice, a set of habits and resources that will keep your idiom skills developing long after you close these pages. This chapter gives you the tools to sustain that practice: resources, communities, goals, and a framework for continuing what you've started.

15.1 Building Your Resource Library: Tools for Continued Learning

The most effective learners don't rely on a single resource. They build a personal ecosystem of tools, some for discovery, some for practice, some for exposure, that keeps language learning alive in their daily routine.

Essential Resource Categories

Reference tools: for looking things up:

• **Cambridge Dictionary of Idioms:** The most comprehensive reference for British and international English idioms, with clear examples and contextual notes.

• **Oxford Dictionary of English Idioms:** Excellent for historical context and formal usage guidance.

• **Merriam-Webster online:** Strong for American English idioms and current usage.

• **Etymonline.com:** Digital learning tools: for building habits:

• **Anki:** Free flashcard application with spaced repetition, arguably the most effective digital tool for vocabulary retention. Create your own idiom deck from this book.

• **Business English Pod (businessenglishpod.com):** Podcast and course platform specifically focused on professional English idioms and phrases, with audio and transcripts.

• **BBC Learning English:** Free resource with dedicated sections on idioms, with audio pronunciation and contextual examples.

• Quizlet: Create or find existing idiom flashcard sets, good for mobile practice during commutes.

Immersive exposure: for naturalization:

• **English-language business media:** The Economist, Harvard Business Review, Financial Times, and Bloomberg regularly use idiomatic language in professional contexts, read actively, noting expressions you encounter.

• **Podcasts in your ind**ustry: Find English-language podcasts in your professional field. Subject-matter familiarity means you focus on the language rather than the content.

• **American and British television drama:** Series set in professional environments, law firms, hospitals, political offices, newsrooms, are dense with professional idiomatic language used naturally. Watch with subtitles initially, then without.

• **LinkedIn articles and executive communications:** Real professional writing from English-speaking business leaders, often rich in idiomatic language in its natural professional register.

Your Personal Resource Plan

The most important resource list is not the one above, it's the one you create for yourself. Take five minutes now to answer these questions:

1. Which one reference tool will I use when I encounter an unknown idiom?

2. Which one digital tool will I use for daily practice (even five minutes per day)?

3. Which one immersive source will I build into my existing routine, a commute, a lunch break, a morning habit?

One tool in each category, used consistently, beats twenty tools used occasionally.

15.2 Engaging in Language Communities: Learning from Others

Language is social: and the fastest path to idiomatic fluency is immersion in conversations with people who use idiomatic English naturally. The resources in the previous section are important, but they are solitary. This section is about the social dimension of language learning.

Types of Language Communities

Language exchange partnerships:

A language exchange is an arrangement where two people each help the other with their respective languages. You help your partner with their English; they help you with theirs, or they are a native English speaker who simply wants to help. Platforms like Tandem, HelloTalk, and Speaky connect language exchange partners globally. Specific to business English: look for partners who work in your industry, the idioms they use will be the most relevant to your professional context.

Professional communities in English:

The most effective immersion is professional immersion. If your work brings you into contact with English-speaking colleagues, clients, or partners, treat every interaction as a learning opportunity. After any meeting where you heard an unfamiliar idiom, note it down and look it up. After any email where you used an idiom for the first time, observe the response. Over time, this turns your professional life into a continuous language classroom.

Online learning communities:

Reddit communities such as r/EnglishLearning and r/businessenglish have active communities of learners and native speakers who discuss idiom usage, answer questions, and share examples. LinkedIn groups focused on business English and professional communication are another active resource. These communities provide a judgment-free space to ask questions, test understanding, and learn from others' experiences.

Mentorship:

If you have access to a native English speaker in your professional network, a colleague, a mentor, a manager, consider asking them explicitly to flag when your idiom usage sounds unusual or when there's a more natural expression for something you've said. Most native speakers are happy to help when asked directly, and this kind of targeted feedback accelerates learning significantly.

How to Get Maximum Value from Language Communities

• Ask specific questions: "Is there a more natural way to say this?" generates far more useful feedback than "Does this sound okay?"

• Bring real examples: "In a meeting today, my colleague said X — what does it mean?" is always more useful than abstract questions.

• Offer something in return: Language exchange is most sustainable when genuinely mutual. Even if your partner's English is strong, offer your expertise in your native language, your industry, or your culture.

• Be consistent: One conversation per week over six months beats intensive sessions followed by long gaps.

15.3 Setting Personal Language Goals: Strategies for Success

Without clear goals, language learning becomes vague and eventually stops. With clear goals, each week has a specific purpose, each month shows measurable progress, and the overall journey has direction.

The SMART Framework for Idiom Learning

SMART goals are Specific, Measurable, Achievable, Relevant, and Time-bound. Here's how to apply this framework to idiom learning:

Not SMART: "I want to get better at idioms."

SMART: "By the end of this month, I will have practiced and used ten idioms from Chapter 9 (team collaboration) in real professional conversations — at least five in writing and five in speech."

Not SMART: "I want to sound more natural in meetings."

SMART: "In every meeting this week, I will use at least one idiom from Chapters 2 or 3 of this book. I will note which ones I used and how they landed."

Not SMART: "I want to improve my business English."

SMART: "Over the next three months, I will work through all fifteen chapters of this book, complete every exercise, and check my answers against the answer key. By the end, I will retake the diagnostic from the Introduction and compare my scores."

Your 90-Day Learning Plan

Month 1: Foundation and Consolidation:

• **Review Chapters 1–5. Identify ten idioms you want to own, expressions that fit your specific professional context.**

• Practice using these ten expressions deliberately, once in writing and once in speech each week.

• Start your flashcard deck. Add five new cards per week.

• Set up your one reference tool, one digital tool, and one immersive source.

Month 2: Application and Expansion:

• Review Chapters 6–10. Add ten more expressions to your active vocabulary.

• Role-play at least two scenarios from Chapter 8, either alone or with a language partner.

• Begin engaging with one language community, online or in person.

• Track which expressions have become natural and which still feel effortful.

Month 3: Specialization and Fluency:

• Review Chapters 11–15. Focus on the chapters most relevant to your specific professional role, negotiation, leadership, written communication, or cross-cultural settings.

• Set one challenge for the month: a presentation, a negotiation, a formal piece of writing, in which you deliberately incorporate idioms from this book.

• Retake the diagnostic quiz from the Introduction. Compare your score.

• Reflect: which expressions are now genuinely yours?

15.4 Reflecting on Progress: Celebrating Milestones

Reflection is not just a nice habit: it's a learning tool. When you reflect on what you've used, what worked, and what felt uncomfortable, you generate insights that passive studying cannot produce.

Reflection Practices That Work

The Weekly Idiom Log:

Each week, keep a simple log with three entries:

• An idiom I used this week: What was it? Where did I use it? How did it feel?

• An idiom I heard or read this week: What was it? What does it mean? Will I add it to my practice list?

• An idiom I want to try next week: What is it? When will I use it?

This takes five minutes. Over twelve weeks, it creates a detailed record of your growth, evidence you can look back on when the progress feels invisible.

The Monthly Progress Review:

At the end of each month, ask yourself:

1. Which idioms from this month's study do I feel genuinely confident using?

2. Which ones still feel uncertain: and why?

3. Did I use any idiom this month that generated a positive response or improved connection with a colleague or client?

4. What surprised me about idiomatic language this month?

5. What's my focus for next month?

Celebrating the Wins:

Language fluency develops invisibly: until suddenly it doesn't. The moment you use an idiom without thinking about it is a real milestone. The moment a native speaker responds to your idiom with an idiom of their own, matching your register naturally, is a milestone. The moment you catch yourself automatically adjusting your idiom use for a different audience, that's fluency developing in real time.

Notice these moments. They are easy to miss because they happen in ordinary conversations. But they are the evidence that what you've been practicing is working.

15.5 The Future of Business English: Embracing Change in Language

Language is a living entity. The idioms that are standard today were new expressions a generation ago. The expressions that are emerging now, from digital culture, global collaboration, and shifting workplace norms, will be standard in the next generation.

How Language Keeps Evolving

Technology continues to generate new idioms at an accelerating pace. "Ping me," "loop in," "async," "bandwidth," and "hard reset" didn't exist as professional expressions thirty years ago. In the next decade, idioms from artificial intelligence, the gig economy, climate change, and whatever emerges from global disruption will enter professional English, and non-native speakers who are already attuned to how language evolves will be the first to absorb them naturally.

Globalization is producing a genuine blending of idiomatic influences. Expressions from South Asian, African, Latin American, and East Asian professional cultures are increasingly entering international business English. This is not dilution, it is enrichment. The English of global business in 2040 will be genuinely multicultural in ways that 1990s business English was not.

The key principle for everything that follows: approach new expressions with curiosity rather than anxiety. Every idiom you encounter that you don't understand is an opportunity, to learn something new, to ask a question, to deepen your fluency. The learners who thrive in evolving language environments are not those with the largest vocabulary. They are those who remain genuinely curious about language, who notice idioms, ask about them, try them, and gradually make them their own.

That curiosity is what brought you to this book. Keep it.

Chapter 15 Practice Exercises

Check your answers in the Answer Key at the back of the book.

Exercise 1: Build Your Resource Plan

Complete the following personal resource plan:

My go-to reference tool for looking up unknown idioms:

____

My daily practice tool (app, flashcards, podcast):

____

My immersive source that fits my existing routine:

____

One language community I will engage with:

____

Exercise 2: Set Your 30-Day Goal

Write one SMART goal for your idiom learning over the next 30 days. Make it specific, measurable, achievable, relevant to your professional context, and time-bound.

My 30-day SMART goal:

____

____

Exercise 3: Your Weekly Idiom Log, Week One

Complete your first weekly idiom log entry:

An idiom I used this week:

____

How and where I used it:

____

How it felt / how others responded:

____

An idiom I heard or read this week:

____

What it means:

____

Will I add it to my practice list? Why or why not:

____

An idiom I want to try next week:

____

When and how I plan to use it:

____

Exercise 4: Final Reflection

Return to the diagnostic quiz in the Introduction. Retake it honestly, without looking at the answer key.

My score at the start of this book: ___ / 30

My score now: ___ / 30

For each expression where your score improved, write one sentence using that idiom in your current professional context:

1. ____
2. ____
3. ____
4. ____
5. ____

Exercise 5: Letter to Your Future Self

Write a short letter (5–8 sentences) to yourself to read in six months. Describe where you are now in your idiom journey, what you're committing to practice, and what you hope to notice is different when you read this letter again.

Your letter:

____

____

____

Chapter Sixteen

Conclusion

You started this book in a meeting, a classroom, or a quiet moment of honest self-assessment, recognizing that idiomatic English was the gap between the professional you are and the professional you want to be perceived as.

That gap is closeable. You've just spent fifteen chapters closing it.

Look at what you now carry: the ability to decode rapid idiomatic conversation without losing your place. The confidence to use expressions from meetings, negotiations, presentations, and leadership contexts, not just to understand them passively, but to reach for them actively. The cultural intelligence to recognize when an idiom is safe to use, when it needs adaptation, and when plain language serves better. A complete practice system, journal, flashcards, role-play, reflection, and resources, to keep developing long after this book is closed.

None of this happened because you memorized a list. It happened because you engaged, with the meanings, the contexts, the nuances, the cultures, and the exercises. Idioms become yours not when you learn them but when you use them. And using them is what you've been practicing throughout these pages.

The journey doesn't end here. Business English will keep evolving. New expressions will emerge. Contexts will shift. Audiences will change. And every one of those changes is an opportunity, not a threat, for someone who has already learned to approach idiomatic language with curiosity, adaptability, and deliberate practice.

One expression to carry with you as you close this book: "You've come a long way."

You have. Keep going.

Chapter Seventeen

Phrasal Verb Glossary

This glossary lists all key phrasal verbs covered in this book, organized alphabetically for quick reference. Use this section when you encounter an expression you want to review, or when you need the right phrasal verb for a specific professional context.

Each entry shows the phrasal verb, its professional meaning, and the primary context in which it appears in this book.

B

- Back down: To reduce demands or concede a position in a negotiation or argument. [Negotiation]

- Back off: To withdraw from a confrontation or reduce pressure on someone. [General]

- Beta test: To trial a product or process with real users before full release. [Tech / Modern Vocabulary]

- Break down: To analyze something in detail; or for a system or plan to fail. [General]

- Break into: To successfully enter a new industry, field, or professional circle. [Networking]

- Break the ice: To ease tension and create a comfortable atmosphere at the start of an interaction. [Meetings / Networking]

- Bring about: To cause something to happen; to produce a result or change. [General]

- Bring down: To reduce something or cause it to fall. [General]

- Bring forward: To move a deadline or meeting to an earlier time. [Meetings]

- Bring in: To recruit or introduce someone or something new. [General]

- Bring on: To cause something to happen. [General]

- Bring out: To reveal or highlight a quality or feature. [General]
- Bring to life: To make abstract data or concepts feel real and vivid. [Presentations]
- Bring to the table: To contribute something of value to a discussion or collaboration. [Team Collaboration]
- Bring up: To introduce a topic into a conversation or meeting. [Meetings]
- Build on: To develop a relationship, idea, or conversation further. [Networking]
- Buy into: To accept or believe in an idea, plan, or concept. [General]

C
- Call off: To cancel a planned event or arrangement. [General]
- Call on: To ask someone to speak or contribute in a meeting. [Meetings]
- Carry on: To continue doing something despite difficulty. [General]
- Carry out: To complete or execute a task or plan. [General]
- Catch up with: To reconnect with someone after a period without contact. [Networking]
- Check in on: To show interest in someone's progress or wellbeing. [Networking]
- Check back in: To return to a topic or person to review progress at a later time. [General]
- Chime in: To add a contribution or comment to a discussion. [Meetings]
- Circle back: To return to a topic, person, or task at a later time. [Meetings / Virtual Communication]
- Close off: To end or shut down an option, discussion, or area. [Negotiation]
- Come across: To encounter or discover someone or something unexpectedly. [Networking]
- Come to terms: To reach a mutual agreement or finalize the conditions of a deal. [Negotiation]
- Come to the table: To be willing to negotiate or participate constructively in resolution. [Negotiation]
- Come up with: To produce or generate an idea, plan, or solution. [General]
- Cut back on: To reduce the amount of something, especially spending. [General]

D
- Deal with: To handle or manage a situation, problem, or person. [General]
- Debug: To identify and solve problems in a process, strategy, or plan. [Tech / Modern Vocabulary]

- Download someone: To quickly brief someone on information or recent updates. [Tech / Modern Vocabulary]
- Draw on: To use knowledge, experience, or resources as a source. [General]
- Draw up: To prepare or write a formal document, plan, or agreement. [Written Communication]
- Drill down: To examine something in greater detail, going below the surface level. [Meetings / Reports]
- Drive at: To be trying to say or suggest something indirectly. [Meetings]

F

- Factor in: To include something as a relevant consideration in a plan or decision. [General]
- Fall back on: To use a backup plan or resource when the primary one fails. [Negotiation]
- Fall behind: To fail to keep up with a schedule, target, or competitor. [General]
- Fall through: For a plan or deal to fail or not be completed as intended. [General]
- Figure out: To find the answer or solution to something. [General]
- Fill in: To provide missing information; or to substitute for someone temporarily. [General]
- Find out: To discover or obtain information. [General]
- Flag up: To draw attention to something important or concerning. [General]
- Follow on from: To be a natural consequence or continuation of something. [General]
- Follow through on: To deliver on a promise or commitment made earlier. [Networking / Collaboration]
- Follow up on: To check on the progress of something or continue a previous discussion. [Networking / Emails]

G

- Get across: To communicate a message or idea successfully. [General]
- Get ahead of: To anticipate and deal with something before it becomes a problem. [General]
- Get around to: To eventually find time to do something. [General]
- Get back to: To respond to someone after gathering information or considering a matter. [Networking / Emails]

- Get buy-in: To gain agreement and commitment from stakeholders before proceeding. [Team Collaboration]
- Get in touch: To make contact with someone. [Networking]
- Get on with: To have a good relationship with someone; or to continue doing something. [General]
- Get the ball rolling: To start a process, discussion, or project moving. [Meetings]
- Get together: To meet up with someone, often informally. [Networking]
- Give away: To reveal information accidentally or intentionally. [General]
- Give in: To surrender or stop resisting; to concede in a negotiation. [Negotiation]
- Go ahead: To proceed with something, or to give permission to proceed. [General]
- Go over: To review or examine something carefully. [General]
- Go viral: To spread rapidly and widely across social networks, reaching a large audience quickly. [Tech / Modern Vocabulary]

H

- Hand over: To transfer responsibility or control to someone else. [General / Leadership]
- Head up: To lead or be in charge of a team, project, or organization. [Leadership]
- Hear someone out: To listen fully to someone's position or concern before responding. [Negotiation]
- Hit it off: To connect instantly and naturally with someone. [Networking]
- Hold back: To restrain yourself from saying or doing something. [General]
- Hold off: To delay or postpone a decision or action. [General]
- Hop on a call: To join a phone or video call, usually quickly and informally. [Virtual / Tech]

I

- Iron out: To resolve difficulties, disagreements, or details. [Meetings / Negotiation]

J

- Jump in: To begin something quickly or contribute spontaneously to a discussion. [General]

K

- Keep in touch: To maintain regular contact with someone over time. [Networking]
- Keep up with: To maintain the same pace or standard as others. [General]
- Kick things off: To begin a meeting, project, or discussion. [Meetings]

L

- Lay off: To make employees redundant; to stop doing something. [General]
- Lay out: To present or explain something clearly and in an organized way. [General / Written Communication]
- Leave out: To omit or not include something. [General]
- Let down: To disappoint someone by failing to meet expectations. [General]
- Link up with: To connect professionally with someone, often digitally. [Networking]
- Look after: To manage or take care of someone or something. [General]
- Look into: To investigate or examine something. [General]
- Loop in: To include someone in a conversation, email thread, or project. [Networking / Emails]

M

- **Move forward: To proceed with a decision or take the next step. [General, used across all contexts]**

N

- Narrow down: To reduce a list of options to a smaller, more manageable number. [General]

O

- Open the floor: To invite others to speak, ask questions, or contribute to a discussion. [Meetings / Presentations]
- Opt out: To choose not to participate in something. [General]

P

- Pass the baton: To hand responsibility to the next person in a sequence. [Team Collaboration / Leadership]
- Phase out: To gradually discontinue or eliminate something over time. [General]
- Pick someone's brain: To ask for someone's informal expertise, advice, or perspective. [Networking]
- Pick up: To resume something that was paused; or to collect or acquire something. [General]
- Pick up the slack: To do extra work to compensate when a team member cannot contribute fully. [Team Collaboration]
- Ping someone: To send a quick message or notification to someone. [Tech / Modern Vocabulary]
- Play down: To minimize the importance or seriousness of something. [General]
- Point out: To draw attention to something; to identify or indicate clearly. [General]

• Press ahead: To continue with a plan or course of action despite difficulties. [Leadership]

• Pull together: To work as a unified team toward a common goal. [Team Collaboration]

• Put forward: To propose or suggest an idea or candidate. [General]

• Put off: To postpone or delay something. [General]

• Put together: To assemble, compile, or create something. [General]

R

• Reach back out: To re-initiate contact with someone after a period of silence. [Networking]

• Reach out to: To contact someone with the intent to connect or start a conversation. [Networking]

• Roll out: To launch or introduce something, often in stages. [General]

• Run by someone: To mention an idea to someone to get their reaction or approval. [General]

• Run through: To go over or rehearse something quickly. [Meetings / Presentations]

S

• Scale back: To reduce something in size, scope, or cost. [General]

• Scale up: To grow a business, process, or operation rapidly. [Tech / Startup Vocabulary]

• Set aside: To reserve time, money, or resources for a specific purpose. [General]

• Set out: To begin a journey or task; to explain something systematically. [General]

• Set up: To arrange, organize, or establish something. [General]

• Share your screen: To display your computer screen to virtual meeting participants. [Virtual / Tech]

• Sign off on: To give official approval or authorization to something. [General]

• Sort out: To resolve a problem or organize something effectively. [General]

• Speed up: To increase the pace or rate of something. [General]

• Stand out: To be noticeably better or different from others. [General]

• Stay connected: To maintain an active professional relationship over time. [Networking]

• Step up to the plate: To take responsibility or volunteer for a challenge when it is needed. [Leadership / Team Collaboration]

• Sum up: To summarize the key points of a discussion or presentation. [Meetings / Presentations]

T

• Table the discussion: To postpone a topic for later (American English) or to bring it up for immediate discussion (British English). Cultural note: this expression means opposite things in American and British English. Always clarify your meaning in international settings. [Meetings]

• Take away: To remove something; or to derive a lesson or insight from an experience. [General]

• Take it offline: To move a conversation out of the current meeting and continue it separately. [Meetings / Virtual Communication]

• Take on: To accept a new responsibility, task, or challenge. [General]

• Take over: To assume control or responsibility from someone else. [Leadership]

• Tie in with: To be connected to or consistent with something else. [General]

• Touch base: To make brief contact with someone to stay connected or provide a quick update. [Networking / Emails]

• Turn around: To reverse a negative situation; or to complete and return something. [Leadership]

W

• Work out: To solve a problem; or for something to develop successfully. [General]

• Wrap up: To conclude or bring something to an end. [Meetings / General]

Z

• Zoom in: To focus on a specific detail or narrow the scope of a discussion. [Presentations]

• Zoom out: To take a broader view or step back from the details. [Presentations]

Chapter Eighteen

Idioms Quick Reference

This section lists key idioms from this book alphabetically for quick reference. Unlike phrasal verbs, idioms are fixed expressions whose meaning cannot be understood from the individual words alone. Use this reference when you want to review an expression or find the right idiom for a specific situation.

A

• A rising tide lifts all boats: When one person or group succeeds, it creates conditions for collective improvement. [Cross-Cultural / Inclusivity]

• **A word to the wise: A piece of advice offered briefly, implying the listener should take note. [General]**

• Above board: Completely honest, legal, and transparent. [General]

• Across the finish line: To complete something successfully, especially after difficulty. [Leadership]

• Agree to disagree: To accept that consensus is not possible and move on while maintaining respect. [Meetings]

• **All hands on deck: Everyone is needed and must contribute, all resources must be deployed immediately. [Team Collaboration]**

• At the drop of a hat: Immediately and without hesitation. [General]

B

- Back to square one: Starting over completely from the beginning after a failure. [General]
- Back to the drawing board: To start a project or plan over completely from the beginning. [General]
- Ballpark figure: An approximate estimate, not an exact number. [Meetings / Negotiation]
- Bang for your buck: Getting maximum value from an expenditure. [American Business Culture]
- Bark up the wrong tree: To pursue the wrong approach or look for something in the wrong place. [Common Pitfalls]
- **Bend but don't break: To remain resilient under pressure, adapting without compromising core values. [Leadership / Change]**
- Between a rock and a hard place: Facing two equally difficult or unpleasant options. [Negotiation]
- Big picture: The overall situation or long-term view, beyond immediate concerns. [Leadership / Strategy]
- Bite off more than you can chew: To take on more responsibility than you can handle. [General]
- Bite the bullet: To accept something unpleasant and endure it without complaint. [General]
- Blow the budget: To spend significantly more than was planned or allocated. [General]
- Bottom out: To reach the lowest point before beginning to recover. [General]
- Break new ground: To do something innovative that has not been done before. [Presentations]
- Bring it full circle: To return to the opening theme, creating a cohesive narrative arc. [Presentations]
- Bring to a head: To cause a situation to reach a critical or decisive point. [General]
- Bury the hatchet: To resolve a dispute and move forward, letting go of past grievances. [Team Collaboration]

C

- Call the shots: To be the decision-maker; to have the authority to determine what happens. [Leadership]
- Carry weight: To have influence or significance; to be taken seriously. [General]

• Caught off guard: Surprised by something unexpected, without time to prepare. [General]

• Chart a new course: To set a fundamentally new direction or strategy. [Leadership / Change]

• Clear the air: To openly address misunderstandings or tensions so they no longer block progress. [Team Collaboration / Conflict]

• Come full circle: To return to the starting point after a long process or journey. [General]

• Connect the dots: To show how separate pieces of information or data link together. [Presentations / Reports]

• Cover all the bases: To prepare thoroughly by addressing every possible angle or concern. [Negotiation]

• Cut to the bone: To reduce something to the absolute minimum. [General]

• Cut to the chase: To get directly to the essential point without unnecessary preamble. [Meetings / Negotiation]

D

• Do your homework: To research and prepare thoroughly before a meeting or decision. [Negotiation / Presentations]

• Double-edged sword: Something that has both advantages and disadvantages. [General]

• Drive a hard bargain: To negotiate firmly and insist on favorable terms. [Negotiation]

• Drive the point home: To emphasize and reinforce a key argument until it is fully understood. [Presentations / Negotiation]

• Drop the ball: To fail to do something that was expected; to make a mistake through carelessness. [Team Collaboration]

• Dust will settle: After a period of uncertainty and disruption, clarity and stability will return. [Leadership / Change]

E

• Easier said than done: Something that sounds simple but is actually quite difficult to accomplish. [General]

• Elephant in the room: An obvious problem or difficult topic that everyone is avoiding discussing. [Meetings]

• Extend an olive branch: To make a gesture of goodwill or reconciliation, especially after conflict. [Team Collaboration / Conflict]

F

• Find a middle ground: To reach a compromise position that partially satisfies both parties. [Negotiation]

• Find common ground: To identify shared interests or goals as a basis for agreement. [Meetings / Negotiation]

G

• Game changer: Something that fundamentally alters the landscape of an industry or situation. [American Business Culture]

• Get off on the right foot: To start a relationship or project in a positive and promising way. [Networking]

• Get the ball rolling: To start a process, discussion, or project moving forward. [Meetings]

• Get the message across: To communicate an idea or point successfully and clearly. [General]

• **Give and take: Mutual concession: both parties offering and receiving something in a negotiation. [Negotiation]**

• Go the extra mile: To do more than is required or expected. [Team Collaboration / Leadership]

H

• Have a game plan: To have a clear, thought-through strategy ready before beginning. [Leadership / Change]

• **Hit it out of the park: To perform exceptionally well, far exceeding expectations. Cultural note: baseball reference, use with care in international contexts. [Team Collaboration]**

• Hit the ground running: To begin something with energy and momentum, without needing time to warm up. [Leadership]

• Hit the nail on the head: To make a point with perfect precision; to be exactly right. [Presentations / Reports]

• Hit the wall: To reach a point of serious difficulty or exhaustion where progress feels impossible. [General]

• Hook the audience: To capture the audience's attention immediately at the start of a presentation. [Presentations]

I

• In a nutshell: In a brief and concise summary. [General]

• In black and white: Clearly stated in writing; or clearly defined with no ambiguity. [Written Communication]

• In hot water: In a difficult or troublesome situation, often facing serious consequences. [General]

• In the loop: Informed and included in relevant communications. [General]

• In the same boat: Facing the same challenges or circumstances together. [Team Collaboration]

J

• Jump on the bandwagon: To adopt a trend or popular activity after it has already become successful. [General]

K

• Keep a level head: To remain calm, rational, and composed under pressure. [Leadership]

• Keep a lid on it: To prevent emotions or a situation from escalating. [Team Collaboration]

• Keep cards close to the chest: To be secretive about your plans or intentions. [Negotiation]

• Keep the momentum going: To maintain the energy, progress, and forward movement already established. [Leadership / Motivation]

• Keep your eye on the ball: To stay focused on the primary goal without being distracted. [Negotiation]

• Kick into high gear: To begin operating at maximum speed or intensity. [Leadership]

• Know the ropes: To understand how things work in a particular field or organization. [General]

L

• Lay the groundwork: To establish the foundation that an argument or project will build upon. [Presentations]

• Lay your cards on the table: To be fully transparent about your position or intentions. [Negotiation]

• Lead by example: To demonstrate through your own behavior the standards you expect from others. [Leadership]

• Learn the ropes: To acquire the skills and knowledge needed in a new situation. [General]

• Let bygones be bygones: To forgive past mistakes or conflicts and not allow them to affect the present. [Team Collaboration]

• Light a fire under: To motivate someone urgently, pushing them into faster action. [Leadership]

• Long story short: To summarize and get to the main point quickly. [General]

M

• Many hands make light work: Tasks are easier and more manageable when everyone contributes. [Team Collaboration / Inclusivity]

• Meet halfway: To make mutual concessions to reach a compromise. [Meetings / Negotiation]

• Mind your P's and Q's: To pay careful attention to politeness, manners, and appropriate behavior. [Cross-Cultural]

• Miss the boat: To miss an opportunity by acting too late. [General]

• Move the needle: To make a noticeable, measurable difference in outcomes. [American Business Culture]

N

• **Not my circus, not my monkeys: This situation is not my responsibility. Cultural note: can seem dismissive, use carefully and only in informal contexts. [General]**

O

• Off the record: Said in confidence and not intended for publication or official use. [General]

• On the same page: Sharing the same understanding; in alignment. [Meetings / General]

• On the same wavelength: Two people who think alike and understand each other intuitively. [Cultural Origins]

• On thin ice: In a risky or precarious situation that could go wrong easily. [General]

• Out of the loop: Not informed about something; excluded from relevant communications. [General]

• Over and above: In addition to what is required or expected. [General]

P

• Paint a picture: To create a vivid, concrete mental image of a situation or concept. [Presentations]

• **Par for the course: Typical or expected in the circumstances, nothing unusual. [General]**

• Pass the buck: To shift responsibility for something to someone else. [Leadership]

• Pat on the back: An expression of praise and recognition for work well done. [Team Collaboration]

• Plant a seed: To leave an audience with an idea that will grow and develop over time. [Presentations]

• Play devil's advocate: To argue the opposite side of a position in order to test it. [Meetings]

• **Pull out all the stops: To use every available resource and effort, to hold nothing back. [Leadership / Motivation]**

• Pull yourself up by your bootstraps: To achieve success through your own effort without outside help. [Cultural Origins]

R

• Raise the bar: To set higher standards; to perform at a level that becomes the new benchmark. [Leadership / Team]

• Rally the troops: To motivate and energize a team before a challenge. [Leadership]

• Read between the lines: To understand the implied or unstated meaning beyond the literal words. [Cross-Cultural]

• Read the room: To sense and adapt to the mood or atmosphere of a group. [Meetings / Presentations]

• Reap what you sow: The results you get reflect the effort and choices you put in. [Cultural Origins]

• Reel someone in: To gradually attract or persuade someone to commit to something. [Negotiation]

• Rise to the occasion: To perform exceptionally well when the stakes are high. [Leadership / Motivation]

• Rubber stamp: To approve something automatically without genuine review or scrutiny. [General]

• Run a tight ship: To manage a team or organization with discipline, efficiency, and high standards. [Leadership]

S

• Seal the deal: To finalize an agreement; to reach the point of commitment. [Meetings / Negotiation]

• See eye to eye: To agree; to share the same view on something. [Negotiation]

• See the big picture: To understand the broader context and long-term implications. [Leadership]

• Set the stage: To provide context and framework before the main content or discussion. [Presentations / Meetings]

• Set the tone: To establish the atmosphere, standards, or culture through early behavior. [Leadership]

• Shake things up: To make significant changes to existing structures or ways of working. [Leadership / Change]

• Show your hand: To reveal your true position, intentions, or limits. [Negotiation]

• Sink or swim: To face a challenge alone, where success or failure depends entirely on one's own efforts. [Leadership]

• Sit on the fence: To avoid committing to either side of an issue when a decision is needed. [Meetings / Negotiation]

• Skin in the game: Having a personal stake or investment in the outcome of something. [General]

• Smooth things over: To make a tense situation calmer, often through diplomacy or small gestures. [Team Collaboration]

• Spark a dialogue: To invite active discussion and questions. [Presentations]

• Spill the beans: To reveal a secret, often accidentally. [General]

• Stand your ground: To maintain your position firmly despite pressure to concede. [Negotiation]

• Stay the course: To maintain direction and commitment despite pressure or setbacks. [Leadership / Negotiation]

• Steer the ship: To guide an organization through a period of uncertainty with control and direction. [Leadership / Change]

• Sweeten the deal: To add something extra to make an offer more attractive. [Negotiation]

T

• Take the bull by the horns: To confront a challenge directly and with courage rather than avoiding it. [Leadership]

• The ball is in your court: It is now your responsibility to take the next step or make a decision. [Negotiation]

• The bottom line: The most important point; the final and most essential conclusion. [General]

• The new normal: The changed state of affairs that has become standard after a major disruption. [Modern Vocabulary]

• Think outside the box: To approach a problem with unconventional, creative thinking. [American Business Culture]

• Throw it out there: To introduce an idea or suggestion into a discussion for consideration. [Meetings]

• Touch base: To make brief contact with someone to stay connected or provide a quick update. [Networking]

• Tread lightly: To approach a sensitive topic or situation with great care and caution. [Cross-Cultural]

• Turn the page: To move past something and begin a new chapter, leaving previous difficulties behind. [Leadership / Change]

• Turn the tables: To reverse a situation, shifting the advantage from one party to another. [Negotiation]

• Two heads are better than one: Collaboration and diverse perspectives produce better outcomes than any single person's thinking. [Team Collaboration / Inclusivity]

U

• Under the weather: Feeling unwell or not at full strength. [General]

• Up to speed: Fully informed and current with the latest information or developments. [General]

V

• Variety is the spice of life: Diversity and difference make experiences richer and more valuable. [Cross-Cultural / Inclusivity]

W

• Walk a mile in someone else's shoes: To try to understand another person's perspective before judging. [Cross-Cultural]

• Walk the talk: To ensure your actions are consistent with your words and stated values. [Leadership]

• Weather the storm: To endure and survive a period of difficulty, uncertainty, or crisis. [Leadership / Change]

• Wear many hats: To have and perform multiple roles or responsibilities. [General]

• When in Rome, do as the Romans do: Adapt to the customs and practices of the place or culture you are in. [Cross-Cultural]

• Win-win: An outcome where both parties gain something of value. [Negotiation]

This glossary covers the essential phrasal verbs and idioms featured throughout this book. For full context, examples, formality guidance, and cultural notes on any expression, refer to the chapter indicated in brackets. The chapter headings and table of contents will guide you to the right section.

Chapter Nineteen

Answer Key

Chapter 1

Exercise 1: Phrasal Verb Meaning Match

1-E, 2-D, 3-C, 4-A, 5-B

Exercise 2: Formal or Informal?

1-I, 2-F, 3-I, 4-F, 5-I, 6-F

Exercise 3: Real-World Application

Sample answers:

1. "I think we need to go back to the drawing board on this one."
2. "I'll follow up on this and get back to you by end of week."
3. "We're prepared to back down on our initial pricing to move this forward."

Chapter 2

Exercise 1: Scenario Matching

1-C, 2-E, 3-D, 4-B, 5-F, 6-A

Exercise 2: Fill in the Blank

1. get the ball rolling / set the stage
   2. on the same page
   3. play devil's advocate
   4. meet halfway
   5. open the floor

Exercise 3: Real-World Role Play

Sample responses: your answers will vary. Look for natural use of the suggested idiom in a sentence that fits the scenario described.

Chapter 3

Exercise 1: Match the Presentation Stage

1-C, 2-E, 3-B, 4-A, 5-D

Exercise 2: Complete the Presentation Script

In order: set the stage / paint a picture / connect the dots / hits the nail on the head / plants a seed

Exercise 3: Write Your Own Opening

Open response. Your opening should include at least three idioms from Chapter 3 used naturally and correctly in context.

Exercise 4: Cultural Sensitivity Check

1-N, 2-S, 3-N, 4-S, 5-N, 6-S

Note: Idioms rooted in American sports: baseball, American football, basketball, often confuse international audiences. When in doubt, pair them with a brief explanation or choose a more universal alternative.

Chapter 4

Exercise 1: Phrasal Verb in Context

1-pick, 2-reaching out, 3-catch up, 4-follow up, 5-loop in

Exercise 2: Write Your Elevator Pitch

Open response. Your pitch should include at least three phrasal verbs from Chapter 4 used naturally in professional context.

Exercise 3: Write a Follow-Up Email

Open response. Your email should include at least four phrasal verbs from Chapter 4 and follow the structure of a professional networking message.

Exercise 4: Cultural Nuance Check

1-A, 2-S, 3-S, 4-S, 5-A

Note: In many Asian, Middle Eastern, and Latin American professional cultures, relationship-building happens more slowly and formally. When in doubt, use more neutral expressions like "get in touch" or "follow up" before moving to more informal ones.

Chapter 5

Exercise 1: Match the Origin

1-C, 2-D, 3-B, 4-A, 5-E

Exercise 2: American or British?

1-A, 2-B, 3-Both, 4-A, 5-A, 6-A, 7-Both

Exercise 3: Safe for International Use?

1-S, 2-N, 3-S, 4-S, 5-S, 6-N

Exercise 4: Origins Research Exercise

Open response. Your paragraph should explain the historical origin of your chosen idiom and connect it clearly to its modern business meaning.

Exercise 5: Rewrite for International Audiences

Sample answers:

1. "This new strategy is truly transformative — we exceeded every expectation."
2. "Let's connect after the weekend and confirm everyone understands the plan."
3. "It's that simple — just submit the form online and you'll have access within minutes."

Chapter 6

Exercise 1: What Does It Really Mean?

1-b, 2-b, 3-b, 4-b, 5-b

Exercise 2: Choose the Right Idiom

1. cut to the chase

   2. barking up the wrong tree

   3. sit on the fence

   4. under the weather

   5. spilled the beans

Exercise 3: Asking for Clarification Professionally

Open response. Your clarification should be polite, professional, and confirm your understanding without disrupting the flow of the conversation. Good responses rephrase what you think the idiom means and invite correction.

Exercise 4: Your One Idiom This Week

Open response. This is a personal practice exercise. Focus on choosing an idiom that fits your real work context and using it deliberately in both writing and speech.

Chapter 7

Exercise 1: Tech Idiom Meanings

1-D, 2-E, 3-C, 4-B, 5-A

Exercise 2: Virtual Meeting Vocabulary

1. take it offline

   2. hop on a call

   3. check-in

   4. async

   5. share your screen

Exercise 3: Old World or New World?

1-T, 2-M, 3-M, 4-T, 5-M, 6-T, 7-M, 8-M

Exercise 4: Tech Idiom Translation

Sample answer: "Hi team, just a note that I have very little capacity this week because of the product launch. I'm trying to fix problems in the presentation while keeping an eye on the client dashboard. Could someone retrieve the metrics from our online storage and let me know when they're available? Let's also completely restart our approach to the marketing strategy since we need something that will spread quickly. Thanks, Alex"

Exercise 5: Emerging Vocabulary Check

Open response. Check that each sentence uses the idiom in a realistic professional context with its correct meaning:
  • Pivot: a strategic change of direction in response to new information
  • The new normal: the changed state of affairs that has become standard after a major disruption
  • Scale: to grow a business or process rapidly and efficiently
  • Async: communication or work that does not require real-time participation

Chapter 8

Exercise 1: Monthly Quiz: Section A (Multiple Choice)

1-b, 2-b, 3-a, 4-b, 5-b

Exercise 2: Monthly Quiz: Section B (True or False)

1-F ("table" means opposite things in American and British English)
  2-F ("bite the bullet" means to accept something unpleasant and endure it, not to make a quick decision)
  3-T
  4-T

5-F (sports-based idioms: especially baseball and American football, are often unclear to international audiences)

Exercise 3: Monthly Quiz: Section C (Fill in the Blank)

1. bite the bullet
   2. burned the midnight oil
   3. circle back

Exercise 4: Design Your Own Role-Play

Open response. Evaluate your scenario against these criteria: realistic setting, clear goal, and idioms that fit naturally in the context you described.

Exercise 5: Your 30-Day Idiom Learning Plan

Open response. A strong plan will be specific (named idioms, named contexts), varied across the four practice types (journal, flashcard, role-play, self-assessment), and realistic given your actual schedule.

Chapter 9

Exercise 1: Team Idiom Identification

1-CR, 2-U, 3-R, 4-CR, 5-U, 6-R, 7-CR, 8-U

Exercise 2: Choose the Right Idiom

1. get buy-in
   2. clear the air
   3. pull together
   4. come to the table
   5. hit it out of the park

Exercise 3: Conflict Resolution Script

Open response. A strong opening statement will acknowledge both parties' perspectives without blame, use idioms naturally at appropriate emotional moments, and end with a collaborative forward-looking invitation.

Exercise 4: Recognition Messages

Open response. Check that each message uses at least two recognition idioms from section 9.3 naturally and that the tone matches the achievement being recognized.

Exercise 5: Cultural Adaptation

Sample answers:

1. "Hit it out of the park", alternative: "exceeded every expectation" / "delivered outstanding results" / "performed exceptionally well"

2. "Bury the hatchet", alternative: "put the conflict behind us" / "move forward and leave the disagreement in the past" / "resolve our differences and start fresh"

3. "Rally the troops", alternative: "energize the team" / "bring the team together and build momentum" / "motivate everyone before the challenge ahead"

Chapter 10

Exercise 1: Email Idiom Selection

1. break the ice
   2. seal the deal
   3. cut to the chase
   4. put all your cards on the table
   5. touch base

Exercise 2: Report Language Transformation

Sample answer: "The project is currently navigating a significant headwind, running approximately two weeks behind schedule due to supply chain disruptions. We have drilled down into the vendor situation and identified production delays as the root cause. To leave no stone unturned, we are actively exploring alternative suppliers to get the project back on track. The bottom line is that despite these challenges, the budget remains within acceptable parameters and recovery is achievable within the current timeline."

Exercise 3: Appropriate or Inappropriate?

1-I, 2-A, 3-I, 4-A, 5-A, 6-I

Exercise 4: Formal vs. Informal Sorting

Formal Written English: "in due course" / "with reference to" / "please find attached" / "for your consideration"

   Informal Written English: "hop on a call" / "ping me" / "circle back" / "shoot me an email"

Exercise 5: Write a Professional Email

Open response. A strong response will use 4+ idioms at an appropriate formality level for senior client communication (neutral to formal, avoid overly casual expressions like "hop on a call" or "ping me"), open warmly, get to the point efficiently, and close with a clear and respectful next step.

Chapter 11

Exercise 1: Negotiation Stage Identification

1-P, 2-PE, 3-O, 4-P, 5-PE, 6-O, 7-PE, 8-O

Exercise 2: Choose the Right Idiom

1. cut to the chase

    2. stay the course

    3. sweeten the deal

    4. hear you out

    5. find a middle ground

Exercise 3: Negotiation Dialogue Completion

In order: win-win / cut to the chase / see eye to eye / give and take / cover all the bases / seal the deal

Exercise 4: Handling the Objection

Open response. A strong response will: acknowledge the concern without becoming defensive, clear the air about any misunderstanding, show genuine interest in hearing the full concern, and redirect toward finding a middle ground or a path forward. Look for natural use of at least three idioms from section 11.3.

Exercise 5: Cultural Adaptation in Negotiation

Sample answers:

    1. "Cover all the bases", alternative: "prepare thoroughly for every possible question or scenario" / "make sure we've addressed every aspect"

    2. "Know when to hold and when to fold", alternative: "know which positions to defend and which to concede, and when to walk away from a deal entirely"

    3. "Roll with the punches", alternative: "stay flexible and adapt calmly when things don't go as planned" / "adjust your approach in response to unexpected developments"

Chapter 12

Exercise 1: Leadership Context Match

1-CM, 2-M, 3-AV, 4-CM, 5-M, 6-CM, 7-AV, 8-M

Exercise 2: Choose the Right Idiom

1. go the extra mile
    2. chart a new course
    3. run a tight ship
    4. the dust will settle
    5. pull out all the stops

Exercise 3: Write a Leadership Address

Open response. A strong address will: acknowledge difficulty without despair, express genuine confidence using specific idioms, set a clear and forward-looking direction, and close with energy. Check that at least six idioms from Chapter 12 are used naturally, not forced into sentences where they feel awkward.

Exercise 4: Leadership Idiom Formality Check

1-F, 2-I, 3-N, 4-I, 5-F, 6-N, 7-N, 8-N

Exercise 5: Cultural Adaptation

Sample answers:
    1. "Step up to the plate", alternative: "take on the responsibility" / "volunteer for the challenge" / "rise to the task"
    2. "Pull out all the stops", alternative: "use every resource available" / "give everything we have" / "hold nothing back"
    3. "Sink or swim", alternative: "succeed or fail based on your own efforts" / "a high-expectation environment where independence is required from the start"

Chapter 13

Exercise 1: Safe or Risky?

1-S, 2-C (baseball origin: may be unfamiliar), 3-S, 4-A (American sports reference), 5-S, 6-A (means opposite things in American vs. British English, dangerous in mixed international groups), 7-C (informal, may seem presumptuous in formal first-meeting contexts), 8-S

Exercise 2: Cultural Communication Style Match

1-B, 2-C, 3-A, 4-D

Exercise 3: Replace the Risky Idiom

Sample answers:

1. "We need to prepare thoroughly for every question or scenario the client might raise."

2. "That campaign was an outstanding success for the marketing team."

3. "Let's postpone the budget discussion until next week." (or "set aside" to avoid the American/British ambiguity of "table")

4. "I think we need to accept the difficulty of the pricing decision and commit to a direction."

Exercise 4: Inclusivity Idiom Application

1. many hands make light work
2. keep an open mind
3. bring to the table
4. a rising tide lifts all boats

Exercise 5: Cross-Cultural Communication Plan

Open response. A strong paragraph will: specify which idiom types to avoid (sports, military, highly informal), note that direct feedback would be reframed as collaborative problem-solving rather than criticism, mention using more formal and universally understood expressions, and demonstrate awareness that in high context culture, what is not said matters as much as what is said.

Chapter 14

Exercise 1: Formality Spectrum Placement

1-HF, 2-N, 3-I, 4-N, 5-HF, 6-I, 7-HF, 8-N

Exercise 2: Wrong Register Identification

1. Problem: "Off the cuff" signals lack of preparation, inappropriate in a board presentation.

Rewrite: "Based on our current trajectory, we are projecting a fifteen percent growth target for next year."

2. Problem: "Cut corners" introduces a negative concept even when negating it, unprofessional in a client proposal.

Rewrite: "We maintain the highest standards throughout every stage of this engagement — quality is central to everything we do."

3. Problem: "Shooting from the hip" is informal and can sound aggressive in a performance review context.

Rewrite: "I'm concerned that some client communications haven't been as carefully considered as they should be — I'd like to discuss this."

Exercise 3: Cliché Alert

Sample answers:

1. "Ultimately, what matters most is client satisfaction." (remove "at the end of the day" entirely)

2. "We should focus on the most accessible opportunities before addressing the larger challenges."

3. "We need genuinely new approaches here — I want to challenge the assumptions we've been working with."

4. "From now on, all expense reports must be submitted within 48 hours." (remove "going forward")

Exercise 4: Recovery Scripts

Sample answers:

1. "Let me rephrase that — I don't mean we're abandoning the project. I mean we've made a strategic decision to redirect our resources based on what the data is showing us."

2. "Apologies for the confusion — 'bite the bullet' is an English expression meaning to accept a difficult decision and commit to it. What I meant was that we're ready to commit to the harder but more effective approach."

3. "I'm sorry — that came out wrong. What I meant was that this particular issue falls outside my area of responsibility, and I want to make sure it gets to the right person who can actually resolve it."

Exercise 5: The Four-Question Framework

1-A (good idiom but "put your best foot forward" may be unfamiliar to non-native Japanese speakers, consider "we are fully committed to delivering our highest quality work")

2-U (widely understood, clear, and appropriate in formal context)

3-A (acceptable but "touch base" may be unfamiliar, consider "connect briefly" or "schedule a call")

4-U (widely understood, positive, appropriate formality)

5-AV (too direct/blunt for a first formal contact in a high-context culture, remove entirely or soften significantly)

Chapter 15

Exercise 1: Build Your Resource Plan

Open response. A strong plan will name one specific tool in each category rather than listing multiple options. The goal is commitment to a sustainable routine, not an ambitious but unrealistic list.

Exercise 2: Set Your 30-Day Goal

Open response. Evaluate against the SMART criteria: Specific (names specific chapters or idioms), Measurable (has a number, how many idioms, how many times used), Achievable (realistic given your current schedule), Relevant (connected to your actual professional context), Time-bound (states the 30-day frame explicitly).

Exercise 3: Your Weekly Idiom Log, Week One

Open response. This is a personal practice exercise. The most important element is honesty, recording what you actually noticed, not what you think you should have noticed.

Exercise 4: Final Reflection

Open response. Compare your diagnostic scores and note genuine improvement. Write sentences using the idioms where you showed the most growth, in your own professional context, not copied from examples in the book.

Exercise 5: Letter to Your Future Self

Open response. A strong letter will be honest about where you are now, specific about what you're committing to, and grounded in a realistic picture of what six months of deliberate practice could produce. Keep it personal and genuine, this is for you, not for anyone else.

One Last Thing Before You Go

You made it. You've worked through 250+ phrasal verbs and idioms, and you're now equipped to follow real English conversations, understand implied meanings, and express yourself naturally in any situation.

I'd love to ask one small favor.

If this book helped you in any way, please consider leaving a review on Amazon. Reviews are how independent authors like me reach new readers. Every honest review, whether it's a quick sentence or a longer reflection, helps another ESL learner decide that this book might be the one that finally makes phrasal verbs click for them.

Your review doesn't need to be long. Just honest.

Share your thoughts here:

sawsancharif.com/review

Scan to Review

Thank you for reading, for learning, and for being part of this journey. I can't wait to share Volume 2 with you soon.

Warmly, Sawsan

Chapter Twenty

About the author

Sawsan Charif is a certified ESL teacher, former United Nations conference interpreter, and seasoned professional with over 25 years of experience as a law firm administrator. Her career has taken her across cultures, languages, and high-stakes professional environments, from international conference halls to corporate boardrooms, giving her a rare, firsthand understanding of what it truly takes to communicate with precision and confidence in English. As both a language expert and a longtime business professional, Sawsan writes from the intersection of linguistic knowledge and real-world workplace experience. 250+ Essential Phrasal Verbs & Idioms for English Fluency is the result of decades spent watching talented, capable people held back by a single obstacle: the gap between knowing English and truly living inside it.